USA TODAY
BOOKS
DOUBLEDAY

TRULY ONE NATION

ALLEN H. NEUHARTH
with Ken Paulson
and Dan Greaney

DOUBLEDAY

Published by Doubleday, a division of
The Bantam Doubleday Dell Publishing Group, Inc.
666 Fifth Avenue, New York, New York 10103

Doubleday and the portrayal of an anchor with a dolphin
are trademarks of Doubleday, a division of
Bantam Doubleday Dell Publishing Group, Inc.

Library of Congress Cataloging-in-Publication Data

Neuharth, Allen.
Truly one nation/Allen H. Neuharth with Ken Paulson and Dan Greaney.
p. cm.
1. United States—Social conditions—1980— 2. Social values—Public opinion. 3. National characteristics, American. 4. Public opinion—United States. I. Paulson, Ken. II. Greaney, Dan. III. Title.
HN59.2.N48 1988
973.927—dc19 88-25800
CIP

(Data applied for)

PRINTED IN THE UNITED STATES OF AMERICA

FIRST EDITION

CONTENTS

CORNER CHAT: Two men spend some time on a bench in Potosi, Mo., the population center of the USA.

INTRODUCTION
THE USA TODAY: HOW IT GOT THIS WAY

The values, traditions and experiences we share weave a similar pattern across the USA. Although many factors make each of us different and special, we are one at heart.

otosi, Mo. Population center of the USA.

Starting point of BusCapade's 50–state tour of the USA.

The Census Bureau calculated that the USA's population in 1980 was evenly distributed around a point near this small city of 2,555 people. Later, amateur researchers from out of town came to a more precise conclusion:

Statistically, at least, our center is on the farm of Lynn and Rosemary Merrill, eight miles northwest of Potosi. In their pond.

BusCapade USA visited the Merrills. Drove down the winding red-dirt road to their house and took a look around the heart of the USA.

▶Stopped by the pond. Oval-shaped, a rowboat pulled up on the banks.

▶Walked past the house. Red brick, neat. A pickup truck parked in front.

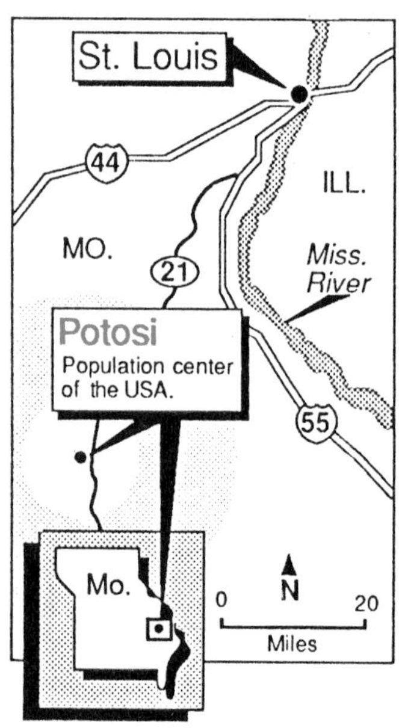

▶Watched the cows loitering along a fence across an open field.

▶Stood on the land. Brown, but greening in early spring.

▶Stared at the sky. Pale blue and big. Stretching in all directions.

▶Talked with the Merrills. Lynn and Rosemary, both 54. He's a farmer; she teaches preschool. Married at 18.

We had come to Potosi to visit the population center. But we were also searching for another center: to see if there was a pattern of shared attitudes, ideas and goals that unites people across the USA.

Before our BusCapade began, I had already visited every state at least once. But never with the time and freedom to really get to know the people and places.

Like most involved in the national media, I have lived for years on the urban East Coast. Dividing most of my time between New York and Washington, D.C. Periodically flying into the heartland with a specific mission and a tight schedule.

I know most of the media suffers from an East Coast bias. Covering the stories that interest people in New York and Washington with only passing thought to the rest of the country. Covering them in a way that reflects the limited Eastern perspective.

And that bothers me.

I had grown up in rural South Dakota. I was losing touch with the grass roots. I thought it important to remember how vast our country is. How diverse our people are. How important their individual ideas and opinions and hopes and goals are.

That was the thinking behind our decision to buy a 40-foot Blue Bird Wanderlodge coach and convert it into a newsroom on wheels.

That was what brought us to Potosi on a chilly Tuesday in March, and across 34,000 miles of highways and byways in all 50 states in the six months to follow.

Looking around the Merrills' farm, we knew we were off to a good start.

No one person, family or town could fully represent everything about the USA, but the Merrills struck a chord. Homey and familiar, they reminded us of a Norman Rockwell painting.

An updated Norman Rockwell painting.

Though rural, they were not isolated or out of touch. A part-time fur trapper, Lynn talked with us about the impact of the stock market on pelt prices. And Rosemary matter-of-factly mentioned traveling to Italy when her daughter was having a baby there.

Past and present. Small town and global village. In one family, the Merrills combined many of the divergent trends and tendencies found across the USA:

►A country family. And a family with children living in urban areas, one as far away as Miami.

►A religious family. And some children who sometimes seem detached from organized religion.

►A solid, long-lasting marriage, and a twice-divorced daughter.

►A family with varied educational experience—one son holding a master's degree in Spanish literature, another who went straight from high school to carpentry.

►Traditional morals. And a modern open-mindedness and acceptance of others' beliefs and standards.

►A love of their home and community. And a son who moved to Texas in search of opportunity.

►Differences, contradictions, but still a family. Divided sometimes by opinion or circumstance, but fundamentally united.

To a striking degree, the Merrills were typical of what we found in six months of traveling across the USA.

We talked to thousands of people. The glad and the sad. The rich and the ragged. The powerful and the poor. The strong and the sick. We came away knowing that these people have more in common than citizenship and language. They share values, traditions, experiences. Some old and enduring, some new but firmly felt.

And from these shared ideas, a sense of acceptance. Of unity.

The barriers dividing groups seem less formidable. Families like the Merrills mix old and new, city and country. Cling to their traditions, but accept the values and beliefs of others.

Partly, the new consensus is a return to pre–1960 values. Partly, it is the incorporation of 1960s' ideas into the 1980s' mainstream of the USA.

Like the Merrills, people across the USA mix old values like:

- ►Country and community.
- ►Faith and family.
- ►Working hard and playing hard.
- ►Dreaming and building.

With new developments like:

►Open-mindedness. The civil rights movement helped make prejudice and bigotry dirty words. They persist, but usually are shunned by most.

►Restraint. After Vietnam, we are less confident about the use of our power, our role in the affairs of the world. The people we met are still very patriotic, but less aggressive.

The lingering impact of these events was visible everywhere as BusCapade traveled the country. The turmoil of the '60s that tore the USA apart laid the foundation for putting it back together in a nobler way. The USA today seems wiser, more mature.

Two trends have helped spread this new consensus:

- ►Increasing mobility.
- ►Exploding media.

In the course of one lifetime, these trends have transformed the USA. Like the people we met on the road, media and mobility have had a shaping influence on my own life.

In 1924, I was born in Eureka, S.D., (pop. 1,200). When I was 11, my widowed mother, Christina, older brother, Walter, and I moved to Alpena (pop. 499).

It seemed likely that I would stay in small-town South Dakota for a long time. And I did.

From 1924 to 1942. I was 15 before I even left the state for three days—thanks to a newspaper boy circulation contest award from the *Minneapolis Tribune*.

I was 16 before I went to Sioux Falls—South Dakota's biggest city, only 120 miles away.

Cross-country traveling was reserved for the rich, who could afford cars or trains, or the rootless, who bummed on the freight trains. Most people stayed near their back yard, except perhaps for a once-in-a-lifetime vacation trip.

Horizons were closer to home.

►One's state was the arena for ambition. Dreams were of statewide success and recognition.

►Entertainment meant shooting the breeze, talking about girls, playing cards or checkers, shooting baskets, playing softball.

►Culture meant waiting and wondering what new movie would come to town on Saturday. Most small-town theaters also showed Sunday matinees.

Some even had a midweek movie on Wednesday or Thursday evening, usually right after the band concert.

►Education meant high school, at most, for most.

►News was a day or two old by the time the newspapers reached town. National events were far away and hard to follow. Radio was the only generally available medium.

Then came World War II. For a generation of millions of young men, and many, many women, war meant hardship, fear and danger—but it also meant a trip away from home. I trained in Minnesota, Texas, Louisiana, California, New Jersey. Served overseas in France, Germany, the Philippines.

Like those millions of my generation, I saw much of my country and the world and liked what I saw.

At home, after the "unconditional" surrenders, my horizons broadened in another way. I was one of 2.2 million ex-GIs to attend college, courtesy of the GI Bill.

Upgraded from my prewar alma mater, Northern State Teachers College, to the University of South Dakota. The student body included ex-GIs from New York and Illinois and Florida and elsewhere. I majored in journalism, edited the student newspaper.

When my first business venture failed four years after graduation, I had a wider sense of my options because of my military experiences. I went south to look for work. To Florida, as far from South Dakota as I could get.

Others went west or east in those postwar years. Or from the country to the cities. From the cities to the suburbs. Many never put down permanent roots, moving with opportunity or their jobs.

Since World War II, we have remained a nation on the move.

At the same time, another development was drawing the country closer together: the communications and information explosion.

►In 1930, 40 percent of households in the USA had telephones.

►By 1960, the figure had risen to 80 percent. Now it's 92 percent.

►In 1930, television had just been invented. But TV didn't come into general use until after World War II.

►By 1950, 9 percent of households had TV sets.

►In 1960, the figure was 87 percent. Now it's 98 percent.

Media and mobility encouraged assimilation. As people from different parts of the country met each other in their new suburban back yards, or saw one another on TV, they became more interested in each other and more like each other.

What happened in one part of the USA could be seen in all parts of the USA. And problems in New York or California became harder to ignore when they appeared in the South Dakota living room.

This became more clear in the 1960s.

Media brought the struggles in the South and in Southeast Asia to homes across the USA. Contributed to the USA's struggle with itself.

Since then the media have helped spread the legacy of these conflicts, the new elements of the USA's consensus.

Media and mobility have fostered national unity in other ways, too. Broken down barriers. Stifled stereotypes. Put people across the USA in touch with national and world affairs. Publicized fads and fashions. Distributed ideas and entertainment, even on the back-most of back roads. From Madison Avenue to Madison, Wis., opera aficionados to football fans, a common culture now unites the USA:

▶Belinda Hughes, 16, a New Yorker transplanted to the New Hampshire woods, said that her new address brought ideas: "I was very surprised when I moved here. I thought the people would be laid-back, like farmers, but they're up on current events. They care about the elections. They care about the Seabrook reactor."

▶David Halladay, 23, hair stylist in Topeka, Kan., spoke to us with his scissors in hand. Said most fads reach the farmlands—at their own pace: "Fashions make it in here from the coast, it just takes awhile."

▶Country boy Lee Stover, 22, Glenville, W.Va., told us modern times have traveled down the country roads that lead to his home. "My parents opened the first video store in southern West Virginia. Now you can stand on your porch and throw a stone at five of them."

Though news and entertainment production is centered in a few coastal cities, all parts of the USA contribute to our common culture. Hardly a day went by that BusCapade did not encounter a famous place or face along the road.

Some of the people and their places:

▶Jack Hemingway, 63, writer and outdoorsman, son of Ernest, father of Mariel and Margaux, enjoys the woods and wilds around Ketchum, Idaho.

▶Margaret Chase Smith, 89, former Republican U.S. senator, casts her light on the small town of Skowhegan, Maine.

▶Bobby Allison, 49, professional race car driver. We met the pride of Hueytown, Ala., out working in his garage after a neighbor pointed the way.

Another tangible testament to our common culture: our chain stores and fast-food restaurants. Though not always the most aesthetically pleasing establishments, they are familiar. Reassuring. Homey. Most of us have been to them. Many of us savor the same favorite meals or burgers.

Safeway Stores, K marts, Wendy's, all provided recurring backdrops for BusCapade interviews. We knew the USA was truly one nation when we drove past the Domino's Pizza store in faraway Fairbanks, Alaska.

Celebrities and chain stores are not the essence of our national character, but they are part of it. A visible symbol of our shared interests and tastes.

McDonald's and Burger King may not be as important to the new consensus as ideas and attitudes, but they give us something in common, something to talk about. And talk we do.

BusCapade USA spent six months asking people across the country what they thought about their lives, their communities, their country, the world. And they told us.

Some out of kindness, some out of curiosity, some just felt like talking. During six months of interviews, only a handful of people refused to talk.

We knocked on doors on country roads and people let us into their homes. Told us their concerns and hopes. Usually offered us a cup of coffee or a glass of iced tea, or lemonade, or a soft drink, or sometimes a beer.

We stopped busy strangers on downtown street corners and they, too, opened their lives and let us in. Harried, hurrying commuters turned into happy and hopeful human beings in front of our eyes.

We saw that city people and country people are not so different. Sometimes they are even brothers and sisters.

We learned that people, black and white, in the city and the country, are usually genuine, and often generous. Given the chance, they are happy to help a stranger. Even a newspaper reporter.

That is the bottom line of BusCapade.

More than any fancy ideas, this friendliness and openness embodies our national character.

Geography, color, politics, philosophies, language—dozens of factors separate us. But overall we are united, because we care about each other.

The rest of this book explores all aspects of our differences and our similarities.

Like the Merrill family of Potosi, our differences sometimes divide us, but we are fundamentally a family united.

The USA is truly one nation.

Allen H. Neuharth
Founder, USA TODAY

1

OUR OWN BACK YARD

We're a nation in touch with the world, but our main priority remains our local neighborhoods. Communities cling to traditions and a strong sense of pride.

PEOPLE POLITICS: Rupert Montague speaks at a town meeting in Bakersfield, Vt., where residents rule and local pride is priority.

ew Hampshire was going to be wall-to-wall politics and not much else.

That's what we thought as BusCapade USA rolled over the border and pulled up to the curb in Nashua.

The tiny New England state's first-in-the-nation presidential primary was less than nine months away. Next-door neighbor Gov. Michael Dukakis was a leading contender for the Democratic nomination. The people were famed for strong opinions forcefully expressed.

Politics, we thought, would be the hot topic of conversation and a handy handle for our profile.

But then we met Judy Thibodeau.

Thibodeau, 39, works as an assembler at a local factory.

"I don't really follow politics," she told us. "I've never gone to any of the speeches or dinners. I don't believe half of what they say. When my family gets together we don't talk politics. Fishing is more important than politics."

Although the mass media have helped in creating an informed, in-touch national community, that's not the whole story.

Though many of our habits and horizons have changed, older ways also endure. Tuned in as the world may be, turned on as its TV sets and radios often are, the focus is still local.

Our personal lives—the private, day-to-day comings-and-goings that seldom make "news" at any level—are far more important than the concerns of the national media and government.

Across the USA, most people were most concerned about the goings-on in their own back yards.

- ▶Family.
- ▶Friends.
- ▶Community.

Of course they want to know about the headlines, national sports events, television specials and money matters. But in street-side conversations almost everywhere, we heard that the nearest is still dearest.

Our non-political New Hampshire factory worker was hardly unique.

In places and states across the USA, we met men and women, even politicians, who recognize that national politics is not everyone's primary concern.

Maryland Gov. William Donald Schaefer understands that potholes on the neighborhood street are as talked about as presidential politics.

"Which is the better job, mayor or governor?" we asked the governor during an interview in his Annapolis office.

"Mayor," responded the governor.

"Do you think you'll enjoy being governor as much ultimately?"

"No."

Gov. Schaefer looked comfortable behind the governor's desk. He seemed at ease in the big office under the Statehouse dome. But he had mixed emotions. He missed his old job.

A Democrat, often described as hard-nosed, Schaefer had come up the ladder rung by rung:

- ►City Council member, 1955 to 1959.
- ►City Council vice president, 1959 to 1967.
- ►City Council president, 1967 to 1971.
- ►Mayor, 1971 to 1987.
- ►Governor.

Where other mayors had floundered in recent gubernatorial races—Koch in New York, Bradley in California—Schaefer won easily. With 82 percent of the vote, the largest plurality in Maryland history.

Most would be pleased to have made it. Many would be aiming higher still. But Schaefer misses the immediacy of the mayor's job.

"As mayor," he told us, "you're right with the people. You belong to somebody. Walk along the street and the senior citizens know you're going to do something for them. Kids know you are going to try to do something. Black people know you're going to try to do something, or at least they can talk to you."

Person-to-person, hands-on, get-the-job-done. Those are the qualities of local politics. Now Schaefer is trying to recapture that immediacy on a statewide level, traveling west and south to remind those far-flung regions of their state connection.

"We've got to sell those people that they belong to Maryland," Schaefer told us. "What I'm talking about is understanding regions of the state as you understand regions or areas in the city, neighborhoods in the city."

Former U.S. House Speaker Tip O'Neill laid down the law: All politics is local.

William Donald Schaefer's style suggests a corollary: The more so, the better.

"I'm a Cherokee Patriot"

Local or national.

Sometimes a sharp division. Sometimes not.

In Tahlequah, Okla., we met a local politician who helps shape the fate of her nation.

The politician: Wilma Mankiller, 41, dark-haired, quiet-talking Indian activist turned administrator. The first woman elected to be principal chief of the Cherokee Nation.

In some ways, her community is like a country. Has its own history, government and language. But is far smaller than even the smallest state. Total population: 78,000.

Independent, but intimate. Mankiller says tribal government is a unique source of strength and continuity for her people. One that predates both state and country.

"Oklahoma is really a new state," she told us. "But we've had our tribal government since the beginning of time.

"My position toward the state is that we have our own government, that we have certain rights and we intend to protect them."

Mankiller—the name derives from an ancestor's military accomplishments—says her tribal identity is especially precious to her because she almost lost it. Almost left it behind.

I think it's possible for an Indian woman to be elected president. But that's . . . down the road. Right now, the tribe is where I'm at. I'm a Cherokee patriot.
WILMA MANKILLER

Two journeys shape her work:

▶A family migration. Because of droughts in the 1950s, the government relocated her family from rural Oklahoma to inner-city San Francisco.

▶A personal odyssey. An increasing awareness of her Cherokee heritage while living in the urban mainstream. Growing activism on behalf of Indian causes eventually led her back to Oklahoma in 1975.

A third journey looms in the background:

▶The Trail of Tears. The 1838 forced march from Georgia to Oklahoma. Destroyed much of Cherokee culture. Created problems that linger to this day. Provided plenty of projects for later reformers.

But Mankiller is upbeat: "I like the direction the Cherokee tribe is going. For a people to survive everything we've survived, there has to be a strong spirit, a strong sense of self. I'm an optimist. I've seen too many good things not to be one."

One thing is certain: her continuing involvement with her tribe. Any ambitions beyond that come later. What about a higher office, we asked.

"I think it's possible for an Indian woman to be elected president. But that's quite a ways down the road. Right now, the tribe is where I'm at. I'm a Cherokee patriot."

Local Flavor

Local food was a recurring theme in our travels across the USA.

Fields of food filled our windows, images of food filled our thoughts through long days of driving.

Food metaphors seeped into our stories as we tried to describe the increasing uniformity of life across the USA. Homogenized. Pasteurized.

But if food provides the words we use to describe our worry about the standardization of life in the USA, food also provides evidence that our fears may be overstated.

In cities and kitchens across the USA, we found ourselves eating things we had never heard of. And liking them. Usually.

At the very least, we learned that table-top USA still retains its local flavor.

►New Orleans. All types of appetites find satisfaction in this Southern culinary capital. Home to two distinct cuisines: Hot, zesty Cajun fare is a crisp counterpoint to the rich and fancy, complicated Creole cookery.

A day's stay in the Mardi Gras city brought numerous delicious diversions:

►Beignets. Deep-fried dough puffs dipped in powdered sugar.

►Community Coffee. A strong local brand with a macho image.

►Etouffee. A spicy, dark sauce.

►Jambalaya. Rice cooked with ham, sausage or seafood and seasoned with herbs.

►Boiled crawfish.

The crawfish weren't yet boiled when BusCapade USA met Bill Racca, 63, setting up for a company picnic on the outskirts of Baton Rouge.

Racca, a Cajun and a weekday maintenance worker, cooks crawfish for profit on the weekend. Uses a 200–gallon tank and a culinary talent he says he inherited from his grandmother.

Bill Racca's recipe for 1,100 pounds of boiled crawfish:

►200 lbs. salt.
►60 lbs. dehydrated onions.
►10 lbs. black pepper.
►10 lbs. cayenne pepper.
►2 gallons concentrated Crawfish Boil.
►1,100 lbs. fresh crawfish.

Bring to boil in a tub of water, add 10 quarts of lemon juice and simmer. Follow those instructions, says Racca, "and I guarantee they're going to be good."

►The special ingredient for Olympia, Wash.'s, famous beer is well-known: two parts hydrogen, one part oxygen.

Paul Decou, 37, blue-eyed brewmaster for Pabst, maker of Olympia beer, told us, "It's the water that makes the difference. It's not too hard, not too soft, and has all the right minerals."

Stephanie Rowe, 18, curly-haired college student, was

even more ardent: "Olympia is famous for its water. It has the best. I don't drink water from anywhere else because it tastes funny."

►Chili means Texas or New Mexico or Arizona to most of us. But chili with spaghetti means Cincinnati.

Skyline Chili, born in a crowded cafe on West Fifth Street in downtown Cincinnati in 1949, is now available at 60 franchised restaurants nationwide. It is still Cincinnati's favorite flavor.

Gail Mahone, 42, secretary, summed up between mouthfuls of "five-way," a mix of chili, spaghetti, cheese, onions and beans: "You have to try it yourself. Skyline is Cincinnati."

►Brian Jooss, 12, Green Bay, Wis., says his state suits his tastes. "I like Wisconsin because it's a bigger state. It's also a dairy state, so you get products like milk and ice cream."

And more than 200 kinds of cheese.

Back Yards Across the USA

From Hollywood to Hartford, from governors to gardeners, BusCapade USA found a strong pattern of pride.

We in the USA care about our communities. We cherish their unique qualities. We like our neighbors.

Whether it's a state or a street, we're concerned about the close-at-hand. Proud of our place. And anything but shy about saying so.

►Vicki Sharoma, 24, dark-haired, stylish Honolulu law student, described her home as "paradise." Said Hawaii's magic never wears off: "I appreciate the weather every single day. It's too beautiful to take for granted. We always say, 'It's another beautiful day in Hawaii.' We never get tired of the sunshine."

►Karl Menninger, Topeka, Kan., famed psychiatrist and human-rights activist, was celebrating his 94th birthday when we talked to him. Responded simply when asked why he located his pioneer psychiatric clinic in Kansas: "I was born here. I liked it. I still like it."

►Phil Deplazes, 46, sells furniture in the unlikely-named town of Cando, N.D. Says proudly that his town lives up to its name: "This town can do, and it has been doing for a long time. It's not easy to stay in business when the crops are down, but small towns are stubborn. We tighten the belt. If we started thinking can't do, we'd be just about finished."

▶Andrew Kovach, 69, blind since birth, sells candy and sings in choirs in the town where he was born, Torrington, Conn. Has no plans to relocate: "I love Torrington. I won't ever leave. They'd only have to haul me back for burial. Why not save them the trip?"

▶Gene Price, 30, welder, Potosi, Mo., summed up an attitude shared by many: "We can crab and complain and holler and murmur, but all in all, if we didn't like it here, we'd be gone."

▶Mary Ann Grub, 36, petite housewife and horse trainer, spoke with us on a bench by Yellowstone's Old Faithful geyser. Said her hometown was another of Wyoming's natural wonders: "Our town is called Eden and it fits. We've got a post office, an ice cream store and three churches. What more do you need?"

Not everyone we met thought their town was Eden.

Complaints sometimes outnumbered compliments.

But almost everyone, almost everywhere had a reason to believe their corner of the country was something special.

Across the USA we found boasting and bragging. My-town's-better-than-your-town one-upmanship. Unabashed boosterism.

No claim was too great:

▶New Yorkers unhumbly called their home The World's Greatest City.

No claim was too small:

▶Folks in Glendive, Mont., claimed fame as The Paddlefish Capital.

Some claims were particularly popular. Literally hundreds of people told us they liked their hometown because:

▶The people are friendly.

▶The weather is nice.

Some of the boosting was an act, an effort to smooth over sore spots when talking to the press.

And some of it was just for fun. Exaggeration for the sheer joy of exaggeration. Tall tales to enthrall the out-of-towners.

But much was simply sincere.

The people really are friendly. The weather usually is nice. And the fact that the same may be said for thousands of places across the USA makes no difference at all.

2 FIRE AND DESIRE

Dedication and determination drive us to strive to win. People across the USA are willing to pay a high price for their dreams.

TIGHT TEAM: Members of Marion (Ind.) High School's championship basketball team huddle to plan strategy.

usCapade USA rolled into Marion, Ind., (pop. 35,874) at midnight on a Saturday in April. Behind the town fire truck.

There was no fire in town. No firemen on the truck. Just Coach Bill Green and the 12 members of the Marion High School basketball Giants.

The fire was in their bellies. In the bellies of the fans who crowded cars and vans stretched out for a mile behind.

It was reflected on the faces of the thousands who lined the streets to cheer the team that two hours earlier had won its third consecutive Indiana high school basketball championship.

►The Giants beat Richmond, Ind., (pop. 41,349) 69–56.

►A year earlier they had beaten Anderson (pop. 64,695) 75–56.

►And two years before, they had started their streak with a 74–67 championship, also over Richmond.

This time the parade began forming as the champs came out of their locker room at the Market Square Arena in Indianapolis, 65 miles away, to head for home.

Horns honking, lights flashing, players waving, the parade crawled through town. Pajama-clad families hurriedly huddled under blankets on front porches. Others gathered on street corners and sidewalks to cheer and wave.

When the parade ended at the high school gym, the 7,500–seat facility was overflowing.

The BusCateers had heard about Indiana high school basketball. We had seen the Gene Hackman film *Hoosiers*. But such devotion seemed almost unbelievable until we attended the Indiana high school basketball tournament.

Watching the hoops and hearing the hoopla in Indianapolis' sold-out arena, we began to be convinced. By the time we reached Marion, we believed.

Steve Tinkle, 18, a Marion senior, testified to the importance of the sport: "Basketball is our whole lives. In the off-season there's a void in our lives. In Marion, you're either on the Giants or for them."

Coach Bill Green sized up the situation in the locker room after the rally: "We're the kings of Indiana high school basketball. We're the kings of Indiana."

It was a proud moment for Coach Green, for his Giants, and for Marion. A sad moment, too.

Nine players on the team had played on all three championship teams. Seven of them would be graduating.

Two of them—Lydon Jones and Jay Edwards, both All-USA team selections—already knew they would be playing together for Coach Bobby Knight at Indiana University. The rest would be going separate ways. It was the climax of an era, and its end. They were the kings of Indiana.

Surrounded by the cheering crowd in the gym, the Giants' victory seemed as though it had been inevitable. Destiny. But destiny hadn't won the games. Hard work, talent and determination had. To play for Coach Green, the Giants had to play by his rules:

▶Two hours of practice each day.

▶A 10 p.m. curfew on weeknights. Except for game nights.

▶No more than 10 minutes of conversation on the telephone each night.

▶Players not allowed to walk girls through the school halls on game days. The unofficial understanding is that players should avoid romantic alliances altogether during the season.

In other places Green's iron rules might be resented. Not in Indiana. Not in Marion. Not after five state championships.

Basketball came up in conversation everywhere in Indiana. Even in the governor's office.

"As far as basketball is concerned," said Gov. Robert Orr, "Indiana likes to think that while basketball was invented in Massachusetts, they learned how to play the game in Indiana."

The heart of Indiana basketball: beating the odds.

The Indiana high school basketball tournament is the only one in the USA with no divisions. Schools of only 150 students compete against schools of 1,000 or more.

Anything can happen.

Anyone can win.

David against Goliath. And sometimes David has a better jump shot.

Marion is no David—its program has been too good for too long for anyone to consider it an underdog—but winning three times straight has a magic of its own. Winning three times straight means you're the best.

The midnight madness in Marion was a unique celebration of one team's accomplishments, but it was also representative of a spirit we saw throughout our trip. The competitive fire in our bellies. The desire to be the best at what we do.

From coast to coast and border to border, this is a nation that likes to win.

Not all competitors or champions slam-dunk a basketball. The fire and desire take many forms.

- ▶Body-beautiful contests.
- ▶Brain-teasing tests.
- ▶Economic competitions between states.
- ▶Vote-seeking from one's peers.

"In Mississippi, They Care About Physical Beauty"

Susan Akin knows the cost of success. Endless, exhausting days. Sacrificed relationships.

Miss America 1986 got her crown the old-fashioned way: She earned it.

Interviewed by BusCapade while we were in her home state of Mississippi, Akin told us that becoming Miss America demanded more than a pretty smile.

A Miss America contestant is tested in four official categories:

- ▶Interview.
- ▶Talent.
- ▶Swimsuit.
- ▶Evening gown.

And one unofficial category: toughness.

Toughness is not a criterion used by the judges to sort out a winner. Indeed, looking or talking tough might contradict the judges' ideas of femininity. But toughness is a factor.

Toughness sorts out the field long before the pageant begins, in the years of practice and competition that go into becoming a serious candidate for Miss America.

"I've been in pageants all my life," said Akin.

She means it. She was 6 years old when she entered her first pageant. By the time she appeared on TV from Atlantic City, she had participated in over a hundred pageants.

Along with her time, the demands of competition also forced her to give up a boyfriend. But not to give up.

Growing up in Mississippi helped her believe that her dream was not impossible. Three previous Miss Americas had blossomed in the Magnolia State. Mississippi's entrants often placed in the top 10.

"In Mississippi, they care about physical beauty," she said. "This past year, in the Miss America contest, eight out of the top 10 were from the South. I think it's because in the South we have a lot of support for the pageant system itself."

Her Mississippi background and plenty of practice gave Akin the edge she needed to win.

Real beauty comes from inside. People who are so carried away with their looks and their bodies—they're going to pass the world by and not enjoy it because they're too wrapped up in themselves.

SUSAN AKIN

Although most spectators focus on the exterior, she feels her victory was more a consequence of her interior. "Real beauty comes from inside. People who are so carried away with their looks and their bodies—they're going to pass the world by and not enjoy it because they're too wrapped up in themselves."

The song at the pageant's end hails the newly crowned Miss America as "our ideal," and perhaps she is.

But not just for the beauty and brains upon which the judges base their decisions. Susan Akin's dedication and drive—and her ability to keep her success in perspective—are the qualities that make her truly a winner.

Some people will do anything to win.

The Constitution requires that a candidate for president be 35 years old and a natural-born citizen of the USA.

Politics require that the candidates ride a corn-picker, attend a chicken dinner and stay a few days with a farm family. And do anything else that might ensure a win in the Iowa caucus.

When BusCapade visited Des Moines, the first-in-the-nation caucus was eight months away. The presidential election was a year and a half away. But in Iowa, the race was on.

The signs along Grand Avenue read like a Who's Who of the 1988 presidential race. Dukakis, Dole and Bush had all set up shop within shouting distance of one another. Others were nearby.

Mike Gearen, 30, came to town from Washington, D.C., to manage Dukakis' Iowa campaign. He compared the political pressure in Des Moines to the East Coast: "You get more of a sense of the campaign here than you do in Washington. If you sit in a hotel lobby for 24 hours and you don't see a candidate, you don't know what they look like."

The election electricity affects Iowans of all types. Lawyers and housewives, Republicans and Democrats pick candidates and pitch in.

Jeanne Hedican, 41, picked Bob Dole. Then she signed aboard as a deputy campaign manager for Iowa. We met her in Dole's Des Moines office, a cluttered storefront with the candidate's name in 3-foot-high letters on the window.

She told us about the prevalence of political passions in these parts. "Politics unites my family. We're all very interested in politics. When there's not a campaign, I'm a mother of four."

David Charles, 36, a Des Moines lawyer, picked George Bush. And not just because of his standing in the polls. Like many Iowans, Charles' involvement in politics goes back a ways.

"I've volunteered for campaigns since 1975," he told us. "I worked for Bush back when I could go down to the airport and give him a ride into town."

Both Hedican and Charles knew what they wanted out of the Iowa caucus: victory. Neither of them expected it to be easy.

"Iowa forces the candidates to go out and meet the people, whether that means going into living rooms or barns," says Hedican. "Iowans don't just sit back in the weeds. They want real answers to real questions. They want to see a flesh-and-blood person eyeball-to-eyeball to see what kind of person they really are."

"I Hate to Lose"

Coach Barry Switzer probably knows as much about the competitive spirit as anyone.

His University of Oklahoma Sooners have won two football national championships and come close year after year.

Success breeds success, says Coach Switzer. Winners want to play for a winner.

Iowa forces the candidates to go out and meet the people, whether that means going into living rooms or barns. Iowans don't just sit back in the weeds.

JEANNE HEDICAN

“We get most of our players from Oklahoma and Texas. Kids who have grown up seeing us win,” he told BusCapade. “We won a national championship while they were in grade school, and when they were graduating from high school they watched us win another.”

Coach Switzer’s players share his feelings.

Dalton Young, 18, grew up near the university in Norman, told us how much he wanted to make the team. How long he had wanted to make it.

“I’ve always wanted to play football for Oklahoma,” said the barrel-chested freshman. “The Sooners were the first team I ever heard of. I wasn’t blessed with any athletic talent, so it’s been an uphill struggle all the way. I’ve been lifting weights since I was 10. I’m willing to help the team in any way I can. Even if it means being a tackling dummy.”

But Young is no dummy. Going into his first year, he had already accumulated a number of college credits. And the maximum 4.0 grade point average.

Schoolwork may be difficult during football season, but Young has his priorities in order. “Grades are more important than football,” he told BusCapade, “because if I don’t keep my grades up, I can’t play football.”

Rotnei Anderson, 21, an OU senior, told us his sports philosophy in the training room while getting ready for practice: “I hate to lose. Everybody in this state hates to lose. We were third in the country in 1986. That’s not bad, but I’d rather be first.”

In Search of Saturn

The Iowa campaigners weren’t the only politicians interviewed by BusCapade. Along with butchers and bankers, housewives and hotelkeepers, we talked with each of the 50 governors in the USA.

No other group of people we met was so obsessed with competition.

Competition in education. Tourism. Attracting industry.

Of all of these, the competition for industry is hardest fought. Education and tourism are important, but winning or losing a factory is a more tangible kind of competition.

Almost every governor described efforts to draw industry. And no other industry or factory was mentioned as much as General Motors' Saturn Corp.

The story?

General Motors Chairman Roger Smith was tired of losing market share to the Japanese. So he decided to do something about it.

In November 1983 he announced a bold new venture to design, manufacture and sell a subcompact car that would meet and beat the competition in quality and cost. Recalling the pioneer rocket program that helped put a man on the moon, he called his idea Saturn.

Smith wanted to remake car-making, from the factory floor to the showroom door.

►Robots and automation were to be used to their fullest potential.

►Relations between labor and management were to be more cooperative and less adversarial.

►A new type of dealership was hinted.

►Every detail of the car-making process would be examined and re-examined. Starting with the location of the plant.

And that's where things became competitive.

When the nation's governors heard about the scope of GM's project—a $3.5 billion construction budget, an estimated 20,000 new jobs—most of them thought they knew just the spot to put the new facility.

Missouri Gov. John Ashcroft thought the Show-Me State could help GM show up its competitors. Mario Cuomo thought GM would love New York. Illinois' Jim Thompson figured that making cars was a natural in the Land of Lincoln. Over 200 sites were proposed.

Saturn became a celebrity.

Enterprising communities went to unusual lengths to attract GM's attention. Some promised tax breaks. Some sent entreating petitions. Others sent flowers.

►Arnold Palmer took a swing at bringing the plant to

Westmoreland County, Pa., with a videotaped appeal to GM.

▶Youngstown, Ohio, assembled a "We Want Saturn" committee with local hero, boxer Ray "Boom Boom" Mancini as a member.

▶Chicago put its pitch on a billboard, and then put the billboard in Detroit. The message: "Saturn Corporation—Chicago Wants You."

And the governors got in on the act. Seven of them even appeared together on the Phil Donahue show to make their pitches in public.

Why the Phil Donahue show? GM chairman Smith was Donahue's other guest that day.

The gestures may have been appreciated, but the affection seems to have been unrequited.

When time came to choose, GM chose a state that had maintained a relatively low profile during the site search. One that made its case based on natural advantages rather than showy salesmanship. Tennessee.

The reasons: a central location, plentiful electricity, a high quality of life, a labor force known for hard work. In sum, a number of factors beyond the control of the governors or communities. Try as they might, the other states could not overcome Tennessee's inherent assets, as then-Gov. Lamar Alexander softly sold them to GM.

Sometimes competition is like that.

Much as we value hard work—luck and inborn abilities can still be the decisive factors in competition.

But that doesn't make competition futile. Tennessee's win was not necessarily every other state's loss.

"The whole process made Missouri a winner," said Gov. Ashcroft. "I sent a letter to 1,500 companies after that and said, 'Look, you've heard about Saturn and what we would do for them. We'll do the same for you.' We have companies that are doing business in the state of Missouri as a result of the Saturn effort. It helped us."

Dollars and development, not just titles and trophies, were the stakes in the Saturn battle. The competition was as fierce as any basketball or football game, but it was fun. And profitable.

Four years later, the USA's governors are still talking about what they learned by pursuing Saturn. Most of all, they learned not to give up.

Like die-hard baseball fans, they called Saturn a building year and looked forward to next season.

"The Whole Ball of Wax"

We were rolling east on Highway 29 when we saw the sign: "Welcome to Bonduel, Wisconsin Spelling Bee Capital."

The story behind the sign:

Seven years ago, Bonduel (pop. 1,100) was just another small Wisconsin town. Not famous for either especially good, or especially bad, spellers.

Then Bonduel students began to dominate the Badger State Spelling Bee, the Wisconsin state championship. They haven't stopped yet.

The state winners, the year and their winning words:

▶LeRoy Perz, 1980, "corolla."
▶David Steuwer, 1981, "canasta."
▶Bob Belke, 1984, "nidificate."
▶Kelly Lecker, 1985, "apolaustic."
▶Eric Johnson, still in sixth grade, won in 1986 with "inferentially."

Myles Belke, 47, the Bonduel math teacher who coaches the spelling bee program, explained the little town's big success in spelling: hard work.

"The student that works the hardest generally wins," he told us.

Winning a spelling bee does not require pre-dawn sprints and double sessions in the weight room, but it does require practice. Lots of practice.

As the state spelling bee draws near, says Belke, the serious speller spends at least three hours each day hitting the books.

Or book. The organizers of the National Spelling Bee publish an official word list, with more than 3,000 entries. Training for the would-be bee-winner means memorizing as much of this list as possible.

When Belke's son Bob was training, he told us, the word list was never far from hand. It even accompanied them on ice-fishing trips.

But work alone doesn't guarantee a spot in the state championship. Only winning does that. And in Bonduel, the winning must start early. Eric Johnson told us that he has been competing in spelling bees since second grade.

In Johnson's case, the training paid off. So much so that Belke wants to enter him in another state championship, though repeat appearances are not allowed in the Badger State Spelling Bee. Belke hopes bee administrators will alter the rules.

Why?

Because winning the state championship is a prerequisite for entering the national championship. And because other states' spelling competitions send repeat winners to Washington.

And because Belke thinks Johnson is Bonduel's best shot at the one prize that has eluded it so far: the national championship.

Says Belke, "He's really got a chance to win the whole ball of wax."

But even if Johnson is not allowed to enter, Belke doesn't anticipate having to take down Bonduel's sign soon. As he told us, "If anybody wants to dethrone us, they're going to have to do a lot of work."

Competition Across the USA

Myles Belke was simply being honest about the work required to beat Bonduel. But perhaps he should have been more careful. To some, his comment might have sounded like a dare. A challenge. And if we learned anything in six months on the road, we learned that the people of the USA respond to a challenge. Dare them, and they'll generally do it.

►Joe Martin, 71, boxing trainer in Louisville, Ky., hands out business cards recommending boxing as a builder of young men's characters. One young man whose character he helped build was Muhammad Ali. Competition is universal, says Martin. "I never met a man there wasn't somebody he thought he could whip. I've turned 71 and I still think there are guys I could whip."

►Ray Thacker, 81, Veradale, Wash., owns and operates an apple orchard. In his time, he was among the best high school basketball coaches in the state.

Out of the game for a few years, one might expect him to be a bit mellow or sentimental. That's not the case.

Talking to us, he berated clumsy apple pickers and ignorant apple purchasers with a vehemence that made us feel for his former players. Curious to see if he had always been so stern, we asked him the secret of his coaching success.

His answer: "If a kid made a mistake, I'd walk out onto the court and tell him that if he did it again I was going to break his arm."

►David O'Dell, 46, manager of the University of Arkansas bookstore and long-time Hogs fan, described his team's goals: "We'd rather beat the No. 1 team than be the No. 1 team."

►Mike Osborn, 40, Denver, told us the competitive fire burns brighter in the rarefied air of the Mile High City.

"This town is Bronco-crazy," he told us, "even when they lose. When we went to the Super Bowl, it was Orange Crush. They painted a big orange stripe down 17th Street and had a parade."

Competition, he says, is part of the Colorado culture: "The Nuggets fans are loyal too. I think it's part of the exuberant spirit of Westerners. It shows the commitment of people from Colorado to work hard and play hard. It's not like San Francisco, where they think they're too sophisticated to cheer."

The biggest, the fastest, the best.

The criteria we used in buying our bus, the aspirations of people we met across the USA.

Companies, candidates and communities go head-to-head day in and day out. Fight to succeed. To win.

Talking to the combatants, we wondered about the

effects of so much competition. After all, a country that idolizes winners might be a hard place for runners-up. And runners-up or also-rans always outnumber winners.

But, as we saw on the road, there's more to life than winning.

There's also cheering.

Competition may divide us—but it also unites us. As we saw across the USA, getting behind our town or team—especially when it's a winner—can involve hundreds, thousands or millions who may never set foot on the playing field.

And as the level of competition increases, ever larger communities unite behind the contestants. Cities, states and regions come together in support of favorite sons and daughters.

Ultimately, competition unites the entire USA. Specific games may divide us, but we are drawn together by a passion for winning.

We share the fire and desire.

3 PAYCHECKS WITH PRIDE

While not all of us whistle on our way to work, for the most part we enjoy our jobs.

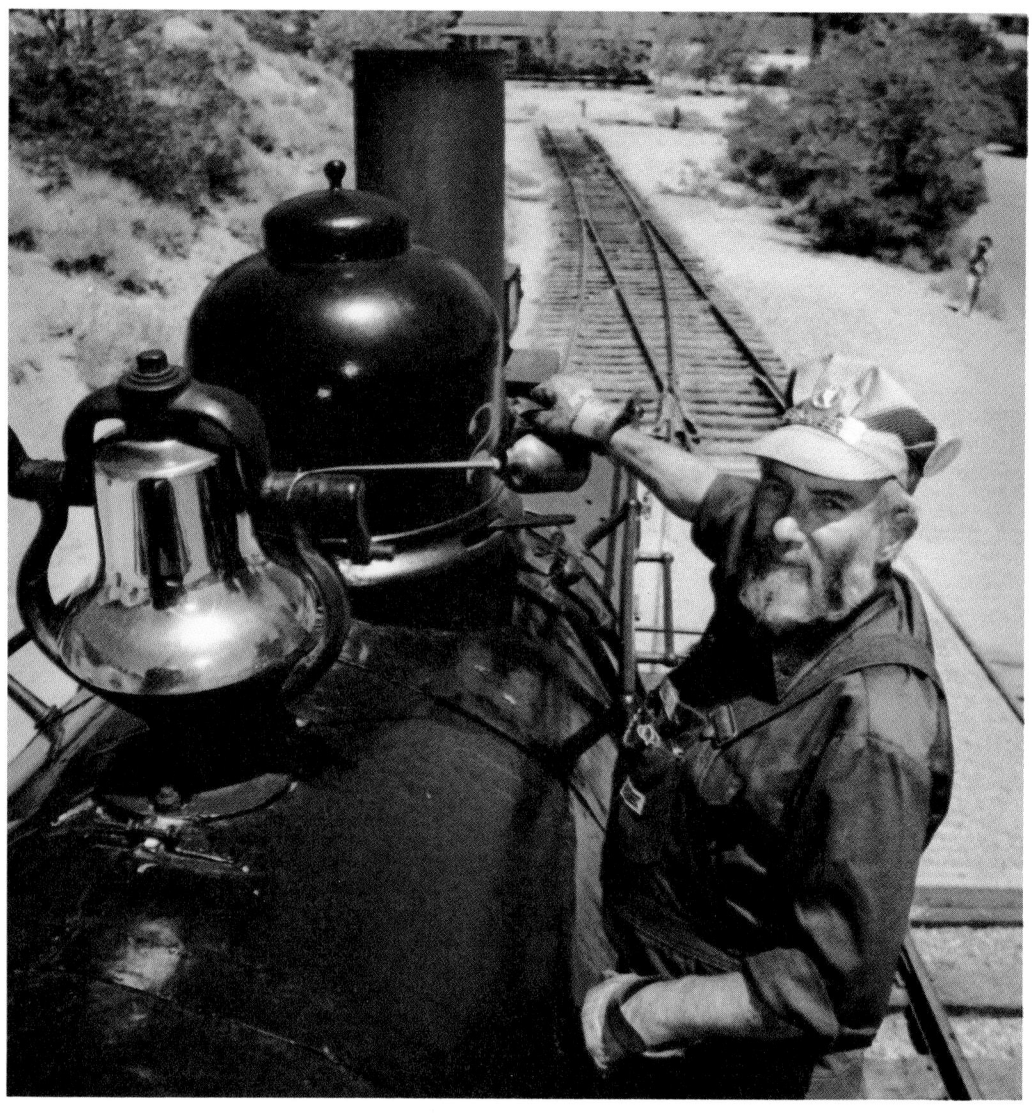

STEAM DREAM: Locomotive engine enthusiast Joe Moore oils his beloved Gertrude, a refurbished steam engine and tourist attraction in Virginia City, Nev.

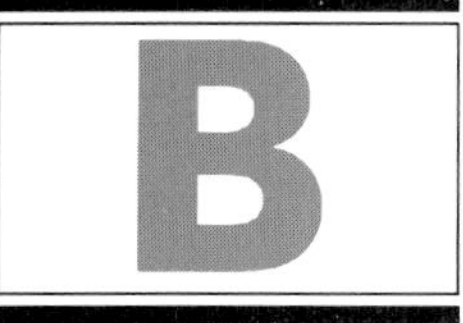

usCapade USA interviewed people at all hours of the day and night. During office hours and off the clock. Heading for home on Friday afternoons. Weekends. Heading for work on Monday mornings.

And we noticed a pattern.

The people we talked to Friday afternoons were usually in a much better mood than the people we talked to on Monday mornings.

Of course, this was no surprise. Everybody knows that everybody loves the weekend. And everybody hates their jobs.

Or do they?

While few shed a tear on Friday afternoon or whistle the company song on the way to work on Monday, hundreds of people across the USA told us they love their jobs.

They may grumble about the pay. Or the hours. Or the boss.

They may not spout sentimental praise for the company on a day-to-day basis.

But most will admit, when pressed, that they like their jobs. Many volunteer it. They believe in the worth of what they are doing. They like their co-workers. Their jobs are part of their identities.

▶That's true in West Virginia coal mines.
▶On Oregon wheat farms.
▶In South Carolina textile mills.
▶In California wineries.
▶On the Alaskan pipeline.

Fun may be too strong a word to describe the attitudes toward work we encountered, but it is not far off the mark.

How else to describe something that produces pride, satisfaction, friendship and, not least of all, money?

"A Coal Miner Is a Coal Miner Anywhere"

It's a dirty job. But Jerry Cornell, 44, is happy to do it.

Like many in West Virginia, Cornell works with coal. Loads 15,000 tons of it onto barges each day for shipment from Huntington down the Ohio River.

Not a job for clean-fingernail fanatics, says Cornell. Coal dust gets into everything. Clothes. Eyes. Mouths. Cornell sneezes coal dust at day's end. Uses dishwashing liquid in the shower.

But he isn't complaining. Jobs can be hard to come by in West Virginia, and loading coal is better than most.

"I feel pretty lucky to have a job in coal," he told us. "It's not the cleanest job, but it's a job and it's steady."

Other West Virginians have an even deeper connection to the coal industry. Hundreds of feet deeper.

The miners we talked to told us they, too, feel lucky to have jobs in coal. One of the USA's most difficult and dangerous industries.

Why do they feel lucky?

West Virginia's hard-hit economy is part of the reason. Another reason is more emotional than monetary.

- ▶Loyalty.
- ▶Tradition.
- ▶Mutual dependence.

Coal mining, we were told, is not just a career, but a community.

Eugene Claypoole, 49, president of District 31 of the United Mine Workers, doesn't work underground anymore. But he did when he was 16. And he says he has never left the community of miners he calls "our people."

Shared danger forges strong bonds, says Claypoole: "There's a strong camaraderie among coal miners. You have to depend on each other. When something goes wrong, you may have to depend on guys 10 miles away."

Dave Gearde, 48, a stocky, dark-eyed miner, agreed. Illustrated the dangers of mining by showing us his scarred legs and arms. Told us of his battle with black lung disease.

Underground, he says, danger makes miners aware of their responsibility to each other.

"You leave your problems at home. You can't dwell

on what's going on outside the mine. If one person screws up, it would affect everyone."

Family ties further unite miners. Claypoole followed several family members into the mines. Says what was true for him was true for many others: "Most miners have fathers who were miners and brothers and uncles who were miners. It's a family tradition."

They acknowledge the mines are wet, gloomy caverns hundreds of feet below ground. And few are satisfied with current safety procedures or job security. But the miners are firmly attached to their work and to one another.

Being a coal miner is more than a job. More than an adventure. It's comparable to joining a family. As Claypoole put it, "A coal miner is a coal miner anywhere."

"She's a Good Engine"

Joe Moore is not an average worker.

If he were, he would work in an office. Or a factory. Or in the hotels and restaurants of the service economy. Not on an antiquated steam locomotive named Gertrude.

Other jobs might be easier, better paying, or just more sensible, but Moore wants nothing to do with them. He is not just another worker, he told us. He is a railroad engineer.

Some people have jobs. Others have careers.

Joe Moore has a calling.

Railroads have called to him as long as he can remember.

Sixty-five years later he looks back fondly at a turning point in his life: "I got my first train set when I was 3 years old. The great moment for me was when I learned how to wind it up myself."

His early life is a story of narrowing the distance between himself and the trains.

His first home in Palo Alto, Calif., was eight blocks from the tracks. Then his family moved.

The new house was only a block from the tracks.

A third move brought them within half a block of the tracks.

Living along the tracks encouraged his absorption. Few trains went by without a wave or shout of greeting. The trainmen, he says soberly, always waved back.

He knew the schedules of the runs between San Francisco and Santa Fe. And of the overnight trains from San Francisco to Los Angeles. He recites the names now, without pausing to recall.

▶The Daylight.
▶The Lark.
▶The Coaster.
▶The Owl.

At night he lay awake in bed and listened for the familiar whistles.

In 1939, at the age of 19, he was finally able to work on the railroad. Worked as a motorman on the Pacific Electric Railway, driving trains throughout Southern California.

Quit in 1943, expecting to be called into the military. Took a temporary job with Railway Express delivering parcels.

Wartime service in the Army included driving trains in occupied Japan. Dismantling ammunition dumps. It would be 30 years until he worked on the railroads again. Worked various postwar jobs until 1978.

Then he met Gertrude.

Knowing Moore's abiding interest in the railroads, a friend in Nevada took him to Virginia City to see the refurbished steam engine being operated as a tourist attraction by the Virginia and Truckee Railroad.

He was impressed. The 1916 Baldwin locomotive was the real thing. A reclaimed log-hauler from the Willamina & Grand Ronde Railway, part of an Oregon lumber operation. Sturdy. Reliable. Steam-powered.

Before leaving for home, he applied for a job.

Since 1978, he has worked for Virginia and Truckee Railroad in Virginia City, hauling tourists back and forth along a two-mile stretch of rail. He drives two miles south, turns around and drives two miles north. Ten times a day. April through October.

"She's a good engine," he says. "Steam locomotives have a soul of their own. Each one has its own personality. If you are romantically inclined, this is a beautiful machine."

And Moore is clearly romantically inclined.

Indeed, romance may be the key to his job satisfaction. Moore and Gertrude, the old-fashioned man and the old-fashioned train, are having an old-fashioned love affair.

"Crafted With Pride in USA"

Textiles are not just made in Greenville, S.C., anymore.

They're crafted. With pride.

So say flags and banners at the Greenville-Spartanburg Airport and at textile factories in the area.

"Crafted With Pride in USA" is the slogan of the textile manufacturers council in its nationwide campaign to persuade consumers in the USA to purchase home-sewn clothes.

The reason: Like so many other industries, textile and apparel makers have been beset by low-cost foreign competition.

▶Between 1980 and 1985, textile and apparel imports to the USA increased almost 100 percent, while the nation's consumption rose 1 percent.

▶In the same period, 350,000 jobs were cut in the textile industry. And 250 plants closed.

Watching these trends, the textile industry resolved to strike back. Bob Swift, executive director of Crafted With Pride in USA, reports that manufacturers have undertaken a variety of competitive efforts.

▶Modernizing factories.

▶Better monitoring of consumer tastes.

▶Closer coordination between retailers and manufacturers.

And, of course, the Crafted With Pride in USA campaign, urging consumers to buy only goods bearing the "Crafted With Pride" label.

We can claim no systematic effort to evaluate and compare U.S.- and foreign-made goods.

But we can vouch for the veracity of the motto.

The textile workers we interviewed in the Greenville area—the capital of the USA's textile industry—clearly do craft their products with pride.

They not only stand behind their goods. They stand in them.

Georgia Smith, 55, inspects cloth at the Woodside Mills plant in Fountain Inn (pop. 4,226). Hunts for defects in the company's acetate fabric that is used in wedding gowns, surgical bandages, even casket linings.

Her rule of thumb: "Our supervisor used to tell us, if we didn't like the cloth, then the customer wouldn't either."

Smith's faith in her wares goes above and beyond the call of duty. She put her daughter's social life on the line. On perhaps the most important night of her high school career.

Says Smith: "I made my daughter's prom dress out of the acetate material here. It was black taffeta. She got so many compliments, and the entire dress cost me about $8."

"We Go From Dawn to Dusk"

Farmers work hard. From sunrise to sunset, and then some.

But times change. Technology has revolutionized farming in the lifetime of most farmers. Chemicals and complex machinery have increased farm productivity while decreasing the amount of labor.

Big corporate complexes have absorbed many family farms.

Combines and tractors with air-conditioned cabs have lightened the labor of getting food out of the ground. But:

- ▶The days are still long.
- ▶The crops always uncertain.
- ▶The weather still omnipotent.
- ▶Financing modern equipment risky.

William Otto, 66, a cigar-chewing farmer in Philips, Neb., is a genuine Cornhusker. He pulled the cigar from his smiling lips to tell us that kids today aren't what they used to be: "When I was a kid, we'd shuck corn for 3 cents a bushel. If you got a hundred bushels a day, you were darn lucky. The young bucks today wouldn't shuck corn for $3 a bushel."

When I was a kid, we'd shuck corn for 3 cents a bushel. If you got a hundred bushels a day, you were darn lucky. The young bucks today wouldn't shuck corn for $3 a bushel.

WILLIAM OTTO

David Birkestrand, 67, farms corn a state away in Cambridge, Iowa. Remembers the good old days. Says these days are better: "Technology has changed farming. The machines came in about the time I graduated high school. That was a good day. Picking corn by hand was hard physical work. It was probably healthy, but I don't know if I want to be that healthy."

Joan Rhinehart, 51, farmer and housewife in Pilot Rock, Ore., was driving a dump truck to the grain elevator when we met her.

Farming may be easier than it once was, she says. But it's still hard enough for her. "Farming is a way of life. You don't plan on a 40-hour workweek. We go from dawn to dusk. We work until the grain elevator closes at 8. The day ends when we get back from the elevator."

The work style has changed. But the rewards remain constant.

►A little money.
►A lot of satisfaction.

Says Rhinehart, "We don't do this to get paid. We own it. There's a sense of accomplishment when you're harvesting."

Others in fields far from farming echoed the Rhineharts.

Some spoke of a sense of accomplishment. Others of pride in workmanship. Or the feeling of making a contribution.

Whatever the reason, the people we met across the USA were clearly working for more than just a paycheck.

►Bob Falkner, 31, Raymond, Ore., says he and his fellow lumberjacks may not be known as Puritans, but they have plenty of work ethic: "People think of loggers as tough, macho, rowdy guys who cuss and chew. But most loggers are just guys who aren't afraid of a hard day's work at a tough job."

The wiry woodsman waxed philosophical: "There's just something inside of you that makes you want to be a logger. I look at a stand of trees and there's a feeling of being in touch with life. It just makes something inside of you jump up."

►Ed Satterlee, 40, Seattle, Wash., is a loyal Boeing consumer. He doesn't buy jets, however. Just builds them and rides in them. The bearded, brown-eyed mechanic says he tells it like this to the airlines: "I always say, 'If it ain't Boeing, I ain't going.' Each jet should have a stamp that says 'Made in Washington.' We take great pride in our jets."

Construction's not for everybody. The first week I worked I was so sore I couldn't bend down to tie my shoes.
LAURIE HEPPER

►Laurie Hepper, 29, Casper, Wyo., was tired and muddy when we met her. She and her crew were hauling away rotten railway ties and laying new track across Wyoming.

The blond, blue-eyed construction foreman told us that her job is hard physical work. But that's OK with her.

"Construction's not for everybody," she says. "The first week I worked I was so sore I couldn't bend down to tie my shoes."

Other hazards: sexist bosses and co-workers.

"It was really awful when I first started. There weren't any women working for the railroad. They said women didn't belong out here. One guy said I should get a waitress job. Some supervisors worked the first women so hard that they quit. I'm just stubborn."

Hepper hung in there. Overcame opposition. Became a supervisor herself.

But perhaps her old opponents were right about construction being man's work. After all, she's got nine of them working for her now.

►Flavio Uribe, 24, San Francisco, has the type of job that children dream about. He's a chocolate maker at the Ghiradelli Chocolate Co. Loves his work, perhaps too much. "I work with chocolate every day, but I still like to eat it. I have a sweet tooth. My fiancee says I shouldn't eat so much. She doesn't want me to get a belly. If I ate as much as I wanted to, I would blow up or break out."

►Darryl Meadows, 44, glass blower in Culloden, W.Va., makes decorative souvenirs, paperweights, art objects. Savors the creative, productive aspect of his work: "I like working glass. It's satisfying. You take a blob of glass out of the furnace and you get to pulling and yanking and twisting and you form it into something."

►Walt Plant, 41, construction laborer, Fairbanks, Alaska, doesn't let cold weather bother him: "People can get used to anything." Plant takes pride in his workmanship. "I came up to work on the pipeline and I just stayed. The pipeline was a real feat of engineering. They brought craftsmen from all over. It was like building the Taj Mahal."

►Jim Hyder, 20, Memphis, Tenn., gives new depth to the word moonlighting.

The younger generation may be as materialistic and acquisitive as the media say. But they are willing to pay the price.

Hyder was getting down to work when we met him—a little past midnight. Told us that coding overnight deliveries at Federal Express' national hub was just part of his busy day. "I also work full time at Memphis State. I work 57 hours a week and I'm carrying a B average. And I'm about ready to get a third job as an umpire in summer league baseball. I get five hours of sleep a day, and I rarely get tired."

One of the fruits of his labor: "I have a 1986 Camaro."

►David Key, 36, Napa, Calif., is a historical anomaly. He keeps on the cutting edge of California culture by practicing an ancient art.

Key is a cellarmaster.

He supervises the making of wine at the DeMoor winery.

In another business, Key says, he might be called production manager. But he wouldn't want to be in another business. He likes being a cellarmaster. He savors the artistry and tradition.

Says: "I enjoy the actual process of making wine. If I were cranking out cast-iron belt buckles, it wouldn't be worth doing."

Away from the job, Moore pursues his interest by

reading from the enormous critical and historical body of wine literature. Wine and wine appreciation have long held a special place in civilized living, says Key: "Nobody writes books about 1948 apples."

Work in progress.

That's what we found while traveling across the country. A nation hard at work in a changing workplace. And changing attitudes toward work.

Backbreaking menial labor still exists, but most workers today earn their pay under far more comfortable conditions than their predecessors did a generation or two ago.

▶The work week is shorter.
▶Pay is better.
▶The work is physically less grueling.
▶In effect, work is becoming more like fun.

Yet there is still hard work and hard workers. Some stay late at the office. Some work two or more jobs. Most give great care to the quality of their work.

The people we talked to were willing to work hard, but most wanted more than survival. For them, work is a source of success, satisfaction and self-expression.

From farming to finance, mining to management, textiles to train conducting, what we do is an important part of who we are. Pride in our products comes as naturally as pride in ourselves or our communities. Pride means as much as our paychecks.

4 HORATIO ALGER LIVES

Ambition and ability to envision the future fuel today's entrepreneurs. Those who want to become their own bosses believe they can parlay good ideas, lots of energy and a little luck into profits.

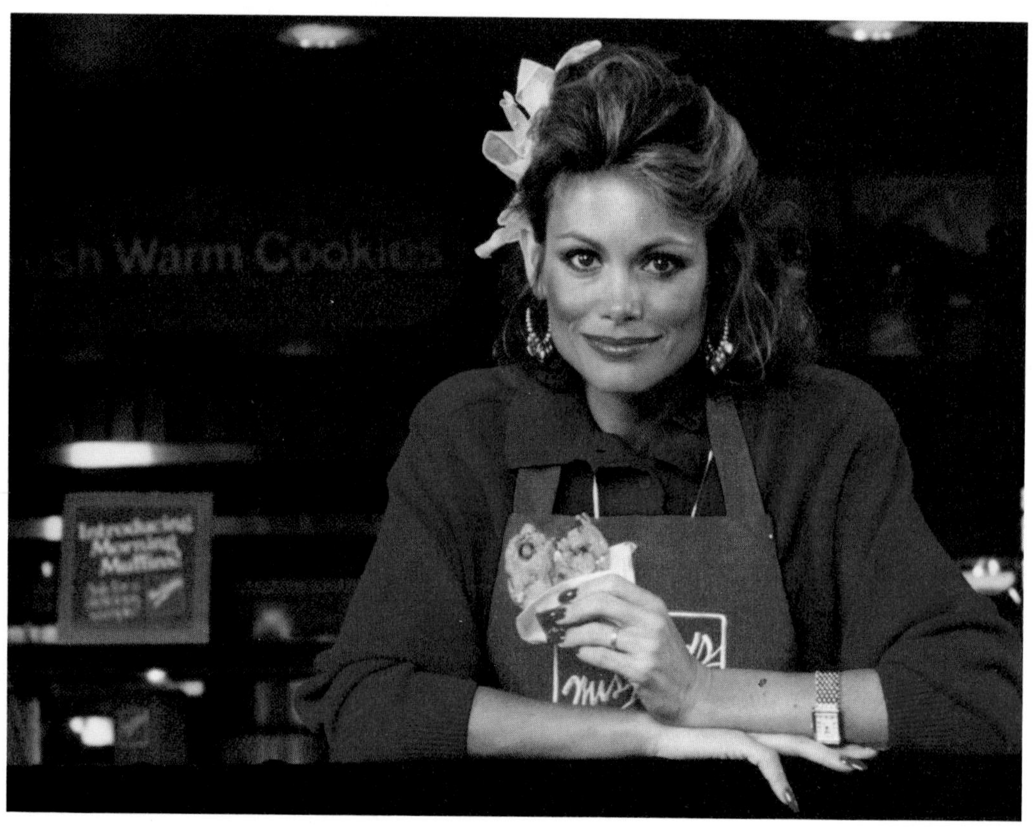

SMART COOKIE: Debbi Fields, at one of her 420 cookie shops, smiles at success.

s we walked the streets of Salt Lake City, we had a sense that something was missing. Litter.

Either all the fast food in Utah is distributed without packaging or this was a city determined to keep things clean.

A pattern quickly emerged.

▶Clean streets.
▶Clean-cut people.
▶Clean living.

A stereotype? Probably.

But a tough one to refute.

Let's face it. Utah is home to the Mormon Tabernacle Choir and the Osmond Family. Not a rebel in the bunch.

What better place for a former Oakland A's ball girl to run a chocolate chip cookie empire?

Her name: Debbi Fields.

Yes, there is a Mrs. Fields behind the $80 million a year Mrs. Fields Cookies.

From the lower level of a shopping mall in Park City, Utah, Fields keeps an eye on her 420 stores in the USA and five foreign countries.

Why Park City?

"We chose to live in Park City because we fell in love with the community and the environment," Fields told us during BusCapade's trip through Utah. "It's a resort community, and people are always in a great mood."

Contributing to that mood is Mrs. Fields Cookies headquarters, the largest year-round employer in town.

Baking is big business. Each year, Mrs. Fields Cookies uses:

▶7 million pounds of chocolate chips.
▶35,000 gallons of vanilla.
▶7 million pounds of butter.
▶10 percent of the world's macadamia nut production.

The ingredients to Debbi Fields' success story:

▶One ambitious 20–year-old who dreamed of running her own business.

▶A first-rate chocolate chip cookie recipe.

▶The courage to ignore those who said her business was bound to fail.

At 9 a.m. on Aug. 18, 1977, Debbi Fields opened her first store at a mall in Palo Alto, Calif. Three hours later, she still hadn't sold her first cookie.

A lesser soul might have packed up her batter and gone home. Not Debbi.

She marched into the streets of Palo Alto and started handing out free cookies.

Folks liked them. Came back for more. Then bought them.

Keep the customer satisfied.

That's Debbi Fields' method and her message.

She shares that philosophy with the store managers who come to Park City for her 10–day cookie college.

"I'm going to teach our managers the values it takes to be successful," she says.

Her recent biography: *One Smart Cookie.*

That's truth in advertising.

Debbi Fields' sweet success reflects an entrepreneurial spirit we saw all across the USA, as more and more people are becoming their own bosses:

▶Business starts total almost 700,000 each year, more than double the pace of the early '70s and about 100,000 more than the early '80s.

▶A USA TODAY poll of the companies identified by *Inc.* magazine as the 500 fastest-growing privately owned firms in the nation found that 89 percent of the owners went into business for themselves because of a desire to control their own lives.

▶Between 1975 and 1985, the number of women working for themselves increased by 75 percent, to 2.8 million. A Small Business Association study predicts women will control half of the nation's small businesses by the year 2000.

We saw that spirit of independence time and again as we visited with entrepreneurs, hustlers and hucksters of the USA.

Their styles vary, but most share the notion that a good idea, a lot of energy and a little luck can take you to the top.

"Domino's delivers."

That's not just a slogan. It's a formula for success.

Michigan-based Domino's Pizza was built on the premise that reliable, quick home delivery is the key to attracting customers.

"It made sense to me almost from the first year I was in business that this is something people want. Service with a capital S," Domino's founder Tom Monaghan, 50, told us as BusCapade traveled through Michigan.

His approach: "Taking it right to their door, and getting it there quickly, hot. Because of the volume that gives you, you don't have to charge any more than if they came to pick it up."

The results:

►The world's No. 1 pizza delivery company.

►Average delivery in less than 25 minutes. (After 30 minutes, there's $3 off on the pizza).

►4,300 stores.

►150,000 employees.

►Projected sales of $2 billion a year.

Monaghan was ambitious at an early age.

While other kids dreamed of playing for the Detroit Tigers, junior high school student Monaghan dreamed of owning the team.

Now he does.

While most kids learned how to turn a double play, Monaghan must have been thinking about turning profits.

Monaghan's empire had the most humble of origins.

When Monaghan was 4, his father died. His mother placed him in an orphanage. Foster homes followed. Later the Marines. Then the University of Michigan.

Dropping out for lack of money, Monaghan bought a pizza parlor in Ypsilanti with his brother.

That single store in 1960 was the launch pad for Monaghan's ambitions. He quickly recognized the potential of campus pizzerias.

Recalls Monaghan: "I had my almanac out and I was writing down the enrollments of every university in the

United States, counting how many there were, how many shops that would be, how much volume I would be doing, how much money I would be making and all the logistics I'd have to go through to get there.

"I was living in a room that I was renting for about $6 a week, and I was thinking about these pizzerias on every campus in the country," laughs Monaghan.

The Vince Lombardi of the pepperoni set. A master motivator.

Many of the company's franchisees started as delivery people or cooks, working their way up to manager and getting some financial help from Domino's to buy a slice of the company.

It's no accident, then, that Domino's ranks include a new generation of entrepreneurs who earned millions by following in Monaghan's footsteps.

Monaghan makes a point of recognizing good work.

If a Domino's store breaks the company's weekly sales record, the manager receives a $12,000 Rolex watch—off Monaghan's wrist.

There are still plenty of opportunities for entrepreneurs across the USA, Monaghan insists.

"I don't think a day goes by when I don't say to my wife, from something I've seen in the paper, 'There's an opportunity for a new business.' Because things are changing, and needs are being created."

But Monaghan warns that pursuing a business dream can require patience and a spartan lifestyle before you can enjoy your success.

His tips:

►Be willing to accept a low standard of living while your business grows.

►Be patient.

►"Wait until the cows start giving milk before you start spending it."

Monaghan says the key is to see your small business as the much larger business it may someday be.

"If you visualize that strongly enough, I think you automatically make the right decisions," says Monaghan.

Just for the record, Tom Monaghan's preferred pizza:

- ►Lots of pepperoni.
- ►Fresh sausage.
- ►Onions.
- ►Extra cheese.
- ►Sometimes bacon, jalapeno pepper.
- ►Delivered in 30 minutes or less.

A Million Glasses of Ice Water

The 18th annual Midwest Trivia contest hinged on this question: "In Amsterdam, the Netherlands, across from Central Station, there is a clock at a stop for the No. 22 bus. Next to the clock is a sign. What does it say?"

The answer: "5,397 miles to Wall Drug, Wall, S.D., USA."

For fans of buffalo burgers and rattlesnake ashtrays, Wall Drug isn't trivia. It's treasure.

There are few better examples of the power of the free enterprise system than this sprawling superstore. Launched during the Depression by a 28-year-old pharmacist named Ted Hustead, Wall Drug Store's first claim to fame was its offer of free ice water to all comers.

These days, Wall Drug serves up more than a million glasses of ice water a year. This fascinating pharmacy off Interstate 90 grosses more than $5 million a year in everything from sodas to souvenirs.

There's wall-to-wall pride at Wall Drug.

Bill Hustead, Ted's son and the 59-year-old president of the company: "We at Wall Drug think it's very noble to be an American businessman or woman. We took a one-room drugstore and built it into the largest drugstore in the world, bringing in $5.2 million a year. But we still serve free ice water and a 5-cent cup of coffee."

A Spud Specialty

At Reed's Dairy Inc. in Idaho Falls, Idaho, Alan Reed has found a new application for the state's plentiful potatoes.

"When my dad told me about the Idaho Potato Commission's big budget for promoting potatoes, I asked him how I could get some of that money to promote a new ice cream product I had in mind," Reed recalled. "He told me to find a way to put potatoes in it. So I did."

His spud specialty: Al & Reed's Ice Cream, available in strawberry, black cherry, chocolate almond and chocolate peanut butter.

"We found that by using potatoes, we didn't have to add refined sugar," says Reed. "That makes our ice cream about half the calories as, for example, Haagen-Dazs."

Reed predicts his product will someday use up to 10 percent of the state's potato crop.

"Of course, we hope to make money," Reed says. "But we hope to do something positive for the state as well."

A Winning Card

B-I-N-G-O.

The aim of the game: profits for the Oneida Indians of Wisconsin.

Since the games' launch in October 1976, the Oneidas' ambitious marketing of bingo has given the tribe growing economic leverage.

Running seven days and seven nights a week, the games draw more than 400,000 players a year from across Wisconsin, Michigan and Indiana.

Profits: more than $1 million a year.

More important, the Oneidas are using the income to launch other enterprises:

- ►A 218–room hotel.
- ►Convenience stores.
- ►A nursing home.
- ►A printing operation.
- ►A gift shop.

Recalls Oneida Indian Chairman Purcell Powless, 61: "Until we had bingo, we couldn't go to a bank and get a loan."

Times have changed.

"Indians are very good at reading signs of the environment," says tribe secretary Gordon McLester, 48. "Two hundred years ago, we brought game back from the woods. Today, we go out in our three-piece suit and deal with E.F. Hutton, and at 5 p.m. we go back into our world."

Entrepreneurs Across the USA

►In Norwalk, Conn., (pop. 80,000), a sign proclaims Stew Leonard's market as the world's largest dairy store. Leonard started out by helping his father on his milk delivery route. Today, more than 100,000 customers a week stop at his thriving store. Near that door is a boulder inscribed with the words that Leonard built his business on: "One: The customer is always right. Two: If the customer is ever wrong, re-read rule one."

►In Dover, Del., (pop. 26,440), Kelly Petit, 27, a collection agent, says his state is ideal for starting your own business.

Says Petit: "I'm trying to get my own business going—refinishing linoleum countertops—and Delaware is a good place to do it. There's very little red tape. Anything you want to do, you just walk in and do it. I can put $50 down and be incorporated on the spot. That's how Delaware makes its money—by making it easy to do business here."

►In Cedar Rapids, Iowa, (pop. 110,243), Rita Van Sickle, 35, owner of a women's clothing store: "I see a trend of a lot of women going into business for themselves. I know women here who have started their own newspaper, an international translation service, a worldwide cookie boutique. We take pride in ourselves and exude that."

►In Thompson, Mich., (pop. 100), Jack Nelson and his wife, Candy, both 42, met the BusCapade team on their 20th wedding anniversary. Jack explained matter-of-factly how they ended up owning their own grocery and gas station. "We camped up here and then the business came on the market. Voila."

I see a trend of a lot of women going into business for themselves. I know women here who have started their own newspaper, an international translation service, a worldwide cookie boutique. We take pride in ourselves and exude that.

RITA VAN SICKLE

Seizing opportunity whenever and wherever it arises. Believing that rags-to-riches is possible, plausible.

For many, Horatio Alger is alive and well. For some he lives in a high-rise in Manhattan and keeps a hectic pace. For others, he runs a bait shop near the Ozarks and sets his own hours.

Whatever the style or personal definition of success, the entrepreneurial flame burns brightly across the USA.

5 DREAMERS

The dreamer's path is paved with strong desire, hard work and a keen eye on the future. Some play the game for fame and fortune. Others reach for higher ideals.

MONUMENT: Ruth Ziolkowski next to model of mountain-size monument her family is sculpting to honor Indian chief in Crazy Horse, S.D.

pportunity appealed to the BusCateers. Opportunity, Wash., a small community on the outskirts of Spokane.

What better place to talk to people about their hopes and dreams?

Brett Renfroe, 19, obliged us.

Married and a machinist in a town with little demand for machinists. Dreams of something more.

"There are lots of opportunities in this country," he says. "You've just got to set a goal and go for it. You can't just sit and watch the world go by. I'm starting out with nothing and I'm going to give 100 percent. I'm going back to school so that I can get ahead."

Renfroe may have a long road in front of him, but not a lonely one. The USA is a nation of dreamers.

We measure our lives in terms of dreams.

- ▶Dream jobs.
- ▶Dream cars.
- ▶Dream vacations.
- ▶Dream girlfriends or boyfriends.
- ▶Dream marriages.
- ▶Dream houses.

On a deeper, more enduring level there is the dream of freedom, progress and upward mobility.

The disadvantaged dream of moving from the margin of society to its mainstream. They hope for a little prosperity, a little security and a little better life for their children.

Others pursue loftier dreams.

Reaching for the stars.

"You Must Work on the Mountain"

Some dreams are inspired. Some are inherited.

BusCapade USA visited Crazy Horse, S.D., on a sunny Saturday in June, in the beautiful Black Hills.

Even then, the winds were high and the roads were rough leading to the mountaintop. We got an idea of how hard life could be here. Made us think of Korczack Ziolkowski.

Korczack Ziolkowski. Sculptor. Connecticut-born, Boston-based. Came to South Dakota in the '30s to work with Gutzon Borglum on the Mount Rushmore presidential monument. Quit in 1939.

But monument-making and South Dakota stayed in his blood.

Approached by Lakota Indian Chief Standing Bear, he undertook a new project. One he would work on for the next 35 years, until his death. And his dream lives on.

"My fellow chiefs and I would like the white man to know that the red man had great heroes, too," the Indian leader had written to Ziolkowski.

The monument-to-be: a mountain-sized carving of Crazy Horse, the Sioux warrior, victor over Lt. Col. George Custer in the 1876 battle of the Little Bighorn.

Construction began in May 1947. Ziolkowski pitched a tent in the wilderness. Started by building a combination home and studio out of logs—by hand. Next were roads and sources of water. Followed by four decades of cutting, clearing, blasting and digging.

By 1982, Ziolkowski and a crew that included his wife and seven of his 10 children had removed 8 million tons of earth. Had started the final carving and polishing of the first section. Then Ziolkowski died.

That could have been the end. But Ziolkowski's last words were an injunction to his family: "Crazy Horse must be finished. You must work on the mountain—but slowly, so you do it right."

Ruth Ziolkowski, 61, heeded his words.

In fact, she says, there was never any question of stopping.

"I'd known my husband all of my life and worked with him since I was 16. He came out here on May 3, 1947, and I came on June 21. I didn't have to make a conscious decision. Crazy Horse has always been my life."

Ruth Ziolkowski and seven of her children were still working on the mountain when we visited.

Dawn, 37, told us her father's dream had become her own. "This place wouldn't be here if it wasn't for the dream," she said.

Ruth and Dawn showed us around the growing complex.

▶Showed us the Indian museum, with more than 2,000 relics from 50 tribes.

▶Told us about plans for a medical training center and Indian college.

▶Showed us Ziolkowski's tomb, which he made for himself at the foot of the mountain.

▶And took us to the top of the mountain.

A white outline of the statue is visible on the rock, an enormous silhouette of Crazy Horse seated on a rearing horse, his arm outstretched to the plains. 563 feet tall. 641 feet long. The eye of the horse alone is taller than a two-story house.

Dwarfed by the scale of the sculpture were the men and women working on the mountain. Day by day they toil on. Year by year. Slowly revealing the figure buried within.

The work is slow. The schedule for completion is open-ended. Mrs. Ziolkowski is sure of one thing.

"I'm certain it will be finished," she said with a look of determination in her eyes. "There are so many people who have faith in the project that it's impossible that it won't be done."

"What Will Become of His Dreams?"

The memorial at the Lorraine Motel, in Memphis, Tenn., reads: "They said to one another, behold, here cometh the dreamer. Let us slay him . . . and we shall see what will become of his dreams."

It was a muggy spring morning when we stopped at the Lorraine, climbed the stairs to the second story and read those words in Room 306. On the balcony outside, familiar from photographs, Jacqueline Smith, 27, a motel clerk who idolizes her hero, pointed out faint discolorations on the concrete. "Blood," she said.

It was here that Martin Luther King Jr. fell after being fatally shot by James Earl Ray on April 4, 1968.

King had come to lead a demonstration in support of striking sanitation employees. Only 39, King already was an international symbol of non-violence and blacks' struggle for freedom and dignity.

►Organized the Montgomery, Ala., bus boycott that led to desegregation of the city's buses.

►Headed pivotal marches and demonstrations.

►Was a driving force behind the passage of the landmark Civil Rights Act of 1964.

►Received the Nobel Peace Prize.

"I have a dream," King told the crowds at the Lincoln Memorial at the climax of the March on Washington on Aug. 28, 1963. "I have a dream that one day on the red hills of Georgia, the sons of former slaves and the sons of former slaveowners will be able to sit down together at the table of brotherhood.

"I have a dream that my four little children will one day live in a nation where they are judged not by the color of their skin, but by the content of their character."

Our visit to the Lorraine came early in BusCapade. Tennessee was our seventh state. That gave us some time to follow up on the memorial's lead and see what has become of his dream.

In Alabama we found new attitudes among those who had opposed King's marchers and the rights they sought to gain.

Joe Smitherman, white, was mayor of Selma, Ala., in 1965. He is still mayor today. But much has changed during his 23 years in office.

Smitherman was mayor when civil rights marchers were attacked and beaten in Selma. He is blunt about his role in those days.

"I was a segregationist," he told us. "I ordered the arrest of Dr. King. I ordered the marches stopped. I was wrong."

He says now he regrets his actions.

"Eventually I grew up," he told us. "We feared change. But when change came it wasn't that bad."

Lorenzo Harrison, black, also lived through history in Selma. He was one of the civil rights marchers.

In 1965, Harrison fought for the right to vote. When he was interviewed by the BusCateers he was an elected government official, the senior member of the City Council.

He is proud of his role in the past, and proud of the progress made toward racial equality.

"The civil rights movement was the greatest movement there ever was," he told us. "Now we have equal representation on the City Council. We have blacks in good jobs—that's something we didn't have in 1965."

The present is not perfect, says Harrison. But he is hopeful for the future. "We know more about each other now than we did then. The whites know more about the blacks and the blacks know more about the whites. I'm not saying we're 100 percent better. We have differences, but we try to work them out for the good."

Across the USA, we saw in reality much of what King could only envision:

▶Blacks and whites sharing tables and meals in Georgia.

▶Children white, black, Asian, Indian, Hispanic able to join hands as friends and equals from Jackson, Tenn., to Honolulu, Hawaii.

▶Racism is stigmatized. In our schools and stores, newspapers and neighborhoods, racist behavior now generally is rejected. Usually. Occasionally it still rears its head.

In Idaho we met a farmer who told a Boston-based BusCateer they shared a sentiment: He, too, was a Celtics fan.

Pleased that someone so far afield should appreciate the world's greatest professional sports team, the Boston BusCateer asked why.

"I like to see the white boys win," the farmer replied.

As disturbing as his statement was the familiarity with which he expressed it—the presumption of agreement. He talked as one white man to another, one good old boy to another.

Racism came naturally to him and, he presumed, to others. But he lowered his voice.

Racism persists in many places, but it lacks the power of law or public approval. It speaks in a whisper.

And back at the Lorraine Motel, we saw a new dream taking shape.

In 1982 the Lorraine was decrepit, neglected, for sale at a bankruptcy hearing. By 1991 it is scheduled to open its doors as home to the National Civil Rights Museum.

D'Army Bailey, a Memphis attorney, is one of the

We know more about each other now than we did then. The whites know more about the blacks and the blacks know more about the whites. I'm not saying we're 100 percent better. We have differences, but we try to work them out for the good.

LORENZO HARRISON

reasons for this turnaround. He raised the money to buy the motel in 1982 and has helped to raise another $8.8 million since to restore the building.

"It struck me as a tremendous waste of a valuable resource," he told the BusCapade, "to do nothing with a place of such enormous world importance."

Apathy, says Bailey, endangers progress toward a truly equal society. "Racism is not dead in this country," he says. "The lunch counters are now open, and we can ride on the buses, but the basic, institutional exclusion from jobs and economic opportunities is still there."

Desk clerk Jacqueline Smith has protested the creation of the memorial in favor of housing for the poor. Still, she says, King's spirit endures.

"The dream is still alive. It's still alive because King's birthday has been declared a national holiday. . . . He made this a country where people are judged by their character rather than their color. What he did affected the world."

Martin Luther King Jr. had a dream. Now much of the USA shares that dream.

"I Want to See My Name in Lights"

Misha Burkhalter, 15, was kneeling on the sidewalk when we met her. Fitting her hand into Marilyn Monroe's concrete palm print.

"I think Marilyn Monroe was so pretty," she said. "I've always wanted to be an actress, ever since I was little."

Welcome to the club, Misha.

Like others before us, BusCapade USA found the air in Hollywood thick with dreams. The sidewalks crowded with dreamers. Especially the sidewalk in front of Mann's Chinese Theatre.

The Walk of Stars is a roll call of greats, past and present. And an inspiration to the would-be stars of tomorrow.

Stars cement their celebrity here. Lasting impressions include:

►John Wayne's fist.
►Al Jolson's knee.
►Hoof prints from Champion, Gene Autry's horse.

Tony Adams, 34, producer of *Victor/Victoria* and *Micky and Maude*, told us that dreams of fame and fortune are part of the Hollywood atmosphere.

"This town is a 24-hour audition," he said. "Everybody's always on. You talk with waiters in restaurants—no one is ever doing what they're doing. They're always just doing this while they're waiting on the big stuff."

His advice to Hollywood hopefuls: "Go for it! If you really want it bad enough and are willing to work hard, you will probably be successful."

Becoming a movie star may not be as unique a passion as carving a mountain, or as noble as leading the civil rights movement, but it is perhaps the quintessential dream. To be rich and famous. Talented and beautiful.

To Richard Little, 32, Hollywood is an open door. We met him at Mann's Chinese Theatre. He works as a doorman.

"I started working here in the hopes that somebody would come by and discover me," he says. "I've been here five years and that hasn't happened yet."

Little may not have the kind of opening he dreamed of, but he's still happy to be in the thick of things. He still feels the romance of Hollywood, the excitement of a movie premiere.

"Most of the time we walk around in a haze," he admitted. "But when we roll out the red carpets, put on new uniforms and have the lights shining in the sky, it recharges you."

Misha Burkhalter needs no recharging. She dreams the old-fashioned dream of glamour, stardom and success.

She wants it all, passionately.

"One day, I want to see my name in lights. In magazines. I want to sign autographs. I want to live in a nice, big, fancy house."

She paused for breath, looked down at the sidewalk and made a vow: "I'll have one of those stars one day."

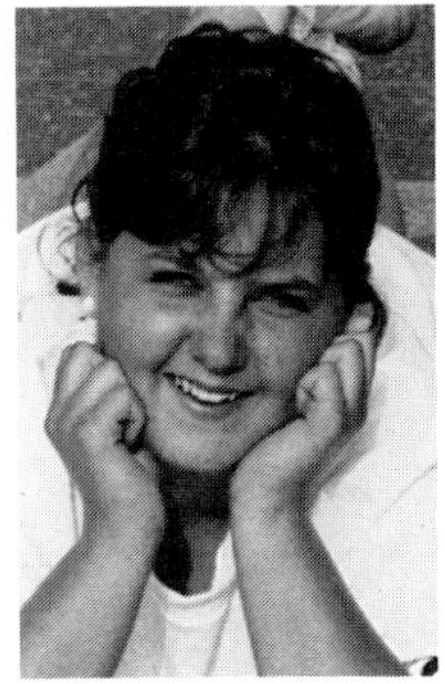

One day, I want to see my name in lights. In magazines. I want to sign autographs. I want to live in a nice, big, fancy house. I'll have one of those stars one day.

MISHA BURKHALTER

Stars were the talk of another town visited by BusCapade. Stars, moons, planets, space stations.

"More vision per mile than anywhere else in the world" is how one resident described Florida's Space Coast. More miles per vision describes the Kennedy Space Center.

►2,411 missiles and rockets have been launched from Cape Canaveral, including 56 manned space flights.

►132 men and women have lifted off from here to explore the universe.

►Accumulating a total of 40,151 man-hours in space.

►The six Apollo launches began their 240,000-mile round trips to the moon here.

►Space Shuttle Challenger took off here on Jan. 28, 1986. Exploded 73 seconds later, killing all seven astronauts on board: Gregory Jarvis, Ronald McNair, Ellison Onizuka, Judith Resnick, Francis "Dick" Scobee, Michael Smith. And Teacher-in-Space Christa McAuliffe.

Since Challenger, NASA has fallen on hard times. Only six successful missions in 1986, fewer than any year since the space program began in 1958. The Soviet Union launched 91 successful missions in 1986.

But don't count NASA out. When BusCapade ended its journey at the Cocoa Beach/Cape Canaveral Space Coast, we found an excited, enthusiastic staff counting down the days until the space program is back in business. Ambitious schedules are planned for 1989 and 1990.

Trim, tall, blue-eyed Mike Parrish, 31, looks like an astronaut, talks like an astronaut, is an astronaut—almost.

Parrish earns his pay as a spacecraft operator and a site test conductor at the space center. "We perform the functional checkouts on the orbiter. We do the countdown exercises. We're the astronauts on the ground. The only thing they won't let us do is clear the launch pad."

And that's Parrish's only complaint about his job.

Although shocked and upset by the Challenger accident, Parrish knows what he would do if given the chance to ride a rocket: "I'd go in a heartbeat. I'd go every day of the week and twice on Sundays."

Dreaming runs in the family, says Parrish. "My whole family is space-oriented. My wife works at the visitor center. My son says he wants to be an astronaut. It's a bond that helps our family out. Everybody wants to reach for the stars."

Despite his earthbound occupation, Parrish still hopes to travel into space. If not for himself, then for his son. He looks forward to the founding of space colonies that will put far more people into space and for a much longer time. Perhaps permanently.

To some this might sound like science fiction. But not to Larry Koile, 56, lead payload technician on the shuttle program. Koile has seen too many miracles to rule out another one.

"Back in the beginning of time somebody built the first canoe and went across the river," he said, tracing man's ventures into the unknown from prehistory to Christopher Columbus to the Apollo landings.

"I want to be there when the next step happens," he paused, and then turned the interview around: "Can you think of anything in history that happened without somebody first having a dream?"

"Spitting Into a Strong Wind"

You'll also find some disappointed dreamers across the USA.

Roger Street, 62, knows about lost hopes. He owns a pawnshop. In Nashville, Tenn.

"We get a lot of people who come here to get rich in the music business," said Street, a heavy man with a slight drawl.

They come to get some of the millions that have been made from country music. The fact that so many country hits dwell on shattered dreams and lost innocence doesn't seem to deter them. They come with big ideas and small resources, says Street. Very little cash, a few songs, a guitar.

He gestured at the acoustic guitars draped around the room. "That's some of it hanging on the walls. They start out with nothing, and by the time they get here, they're minus."

The pawnshop stands just a few blocks from the old Ryman Auditorium, longtime home of the nationally famous Grand Ole Opry country music radio program. But when the Grand Ole Opry moved 10 miles east and turned into a theme park called Opryland, this neighborhood stayed put. Between the bars and boarded store fronts, some music-related businesses linger, including a vintage guitar store and several record stores. But it is the pawnshop that strikes the telling chord, the mix of dreams and despondency.

"They were going to get rich," says Street about his customers. He shrugs. "It's spitting into a strong wind."

Other disappointed dreamers:

▶Clifford Blalock, 43, Commanche, Okla., watched his modest dream slip away when crop prices dropped and his mortgage payments came due. "There isn't any money in circulation in farming anymore," he told us. "It's getting hard to make a living. I've farmed all my life, and I lost my farm—the bank closed on it. I worked the last 20 years to pay for a home and then I lost it."

▶Frank Hoffman, Menominee, Wis., is no ancient mariner, but he has his albatross to contend with—a century-old, 113-foot, 210-ton formerly sunken schooner.

Hoffman discovered the ship in 1969 and raised it from the lake bottom with the dream of turning it into a thriving tourist attraction. But few tourists showed up.

In June 1985, a frustrated, whiskey-soaked Hoffman put a torch to the ship. He tried to hold police and firemen at bay with a rifle. Was given a suspended sentence on arson and assault charges and told to seek help for a drinking problem.

"I owe $300,000," Hoffman told a BusCapade reporter. "I've tried every state and national representative, the National Trust, the maritime preservation people. There's no help for me."

Since our visit, Hoffman's fortunes improved a bit. He sold the ship and moved to Florida.

Most of the dreams and dreamers we met were more fortunate.

Many were more concerned with making their dreams real than with talking about them. They were going to school, doing their homework, laying the foundations for their castles in the air.

►Sara Dorner, 13, Green Bay, Wis., has a plan. She knows that fame, fortune and success require practical steps. Her first will be getting her driver's license. Turning 16 is her dream now, she says, "So I can drive to New York and be a dancer."

►Jack Brickhouse knows all about dreaming. As play-by-play man for the Chicago Cubs for more than 40 years before his retirement, he's had a lot of practice at it. We asked the Hall of Fame broadcaster what kept him going when his Cubs were 20 games behind. "If you really look for the positive, you can find it."

And, like all dreamers, you look toward the future. "You're talking to the eternal optimist," he told us. "The way baseball is today, two or three kids could turn a club around. You can have a last-place club, but one or two guys coming around can make a difference. That could happen this year."

►Jerry Schneidman, 42, a teacher in the Bronx, is no dreamer. Or so he says. When we met him coming out of Bally's casino in Atlantic City, he scoffed at the thought of striking it rich.

A trip to the seashore, a little bit of light and air, some fun for his mother—these were his reasons for traveling to the resort.

"You come out here expecting to make a donation," he said. "But the idea of hitting a jackpot is always on my mind."

Glancing around at the bustling crowd and at his mother, seated, smiling, on a nearby bench, he decided that perhaps foolish dreams aren't so foolish. "This place is made on fantasy," he said. "If you take away people's fantasies you're not doing them a favor."

►Debbie Brown, a prostitute at the Mustang Ranch, one of Nevada's legal brothels outside Reno, told us her ambitions. "I'm going for the American dream. I'm trying to put together a down payment on a house and buy a second car. I want to see my 4-month-old daughter, Jennifer, go to school and be something better than I ever was."

▶Monica Kuljich, 22, is a native of Lima, Peru, who has lived in Miami for five years. A petite woman with hazel eyes and frosted blond hair, she is a saleswoman in a jewelry store.

She apologized for her accent, but her voice was crystal clear: "There are more opportunities here, in America, than there are in my country. Anything you want is possible. A person like me, who comes here with nothing, can make it in three years. In my country it would take at least 20. This is the country of dreams. If you dream it, believe it, and work hard for it, one day you can take your dream by the hand and run with it."

6 THROUGH THICK AND THIN

Hope stays in our hearts. People, realistic about setbacks and sacrifices, change to meet new challenges. Overcome hardship and heartache. Adapt to adversity without abandoning goals.

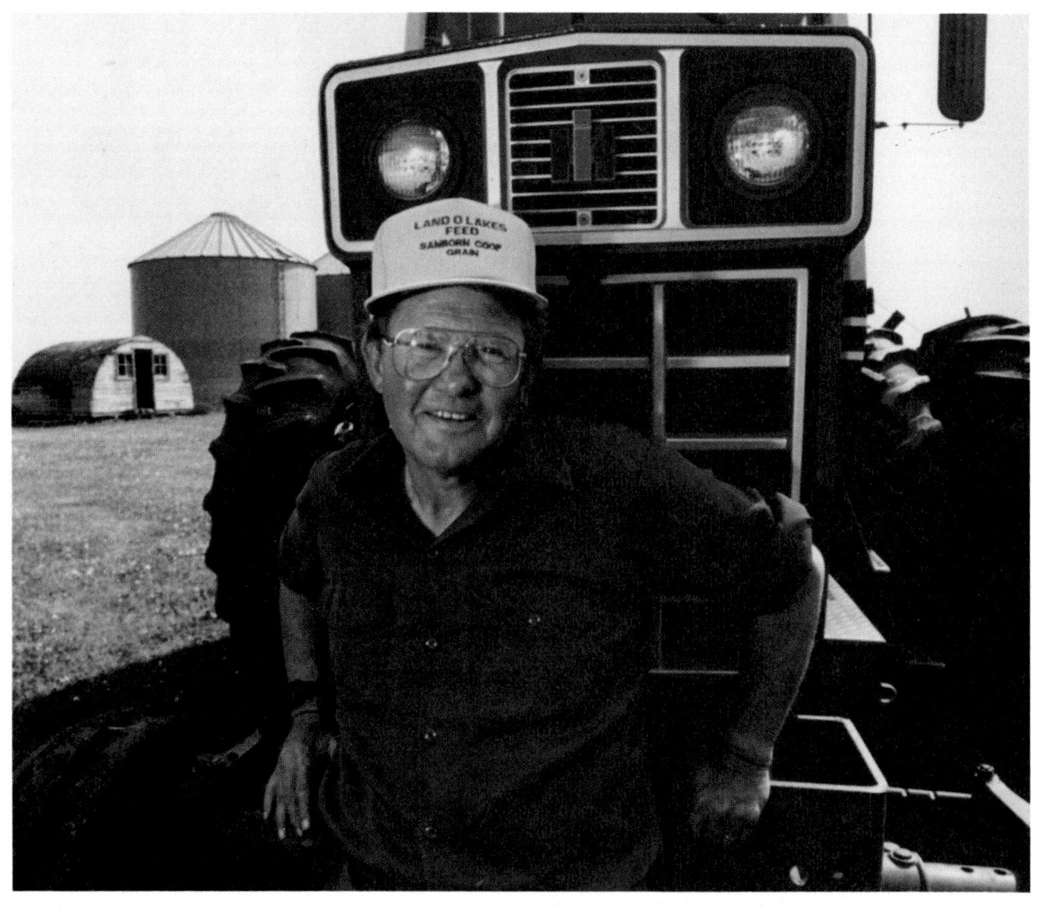

FARM CHARM: Howard Postma of Sanborn, Iowa, in front of tractor he uses on his farm.

oward Postma, 55, Sanborn, Iowa, surprised the Bus-Capade.

But first we surprised him.

Postma hadn't planned on being interviewed on the June morning that we met him. He had planned on getting some weeding done.

And that's what he was doing when we spotted him. We pulled over, flagged down his red and white tractor with a green and white canopy, climbed over his fence, walked across his field and began asking him questions about life and farming in Iowa.

That's when he surprised us.

Farm failures and foreclosures have been the big story from the heartland for five years. We expected farmers to tell us about hardship and heartache. Despair and despondency.

Not Howard Postma.

He talked to us about debt management, competitiveness, crop diversification. About technology and modernization. About the need to run a farm like a business.

"The farmer is not a clodhopper anymore," he told us.

We found his sentiments echoed on farms and fields throughout our trip.

Many have been forced out of farming forever, but those who remain are more savvy and sophisticated than their predecessors. They have to be.

Farming has changed. And farmers have changed with it.

And the farmers aren't alone.

Across the USA, across all types of employment, we met people who were adapting and changing to meet the challenges they face. No one welcomes trouble, but few abandon hope in the face of hardship. Some are shocked and shattered. Some cannot adapt. But we found a surprising number of people fighting back:

▶Surviving.
▶Struggling.
▶Succeeding.

"Oil's Going to Come Back"

When oil went down, it took a lot of people with it.

Not just oilmen, and not just in Texas.

Housewives and high school students, bankers and brokers suffered along with their oil-employed parents and spouses, customers and creditors.

We met these boom-and-busters from Oklahoma to North Dakota. Heard about bankruptcies, repossessions, unemployment. Fear and hope. Mostly about hope.

Oil prices were one cause. Price per barrel for West Texas intermediate crude neared $20 while we were on the road. Down from a high of $40, but up from a low of $12.

Oil people were the other reason for hope. Always an all-or-nothing enterprise, oil seems to attract optimists. Realistic about sacrifices and setbacks. But romantic enough to dream of booms to come.

▶Gia Rummery, 24, Enid, Okla., cooks and waits tables for her pay but has a wildcatter's gift for great expectations. Looks on the bright side of the current slump: "We've got brand new houses, sitting empty. If they start drilling oil again, we'd really be on our way. All of those houses are just waiting to be occupied. The people coming to town for oil jobs could just move right in."

▶Lois Schwarzenberger, 41, Grassy Butte, N.D., brown-haired, jeans-wearing homemaker, works part time in the post office to make ends meet: "My husband used to work in the oil field, but he got laid off. Now he does odd jobs around town, helping neighbors put in a crop or brand calves."

Less money means less of everything, including luxuries many of us consider necessities: "We don't have a telephone. We're too broke. And we don't drive to visit as much as we used to, because we have to watch the gas. We're dealing with it, but we hope things turn around."

▶Spencer Philo, 19, student, Casper, Wyo., has been around oil all his life. He watched it go down but is betting his future that it will come back up.

"I worked in the oil fields with my dad as a pumper, then the company went under," he told us. "I'm majoring in petroleum engineering. There's only three of us in my class. But they say not to let anybody talk you out of it. Oil's going to come back."

A Regimen of Hope

1964 Olympic medalist Jimmy Heuga, 43, skis 45 days each winter. Bicycles 15 miles every day. Usually swims a mile, too.

Not unusual for a resident of a Colorado ski town.

Very unusual for a man with multiple sclerosis, the degenerative disease of the nervous system that saps strength and coordination.

In 1964, Heuga won the bronze medal for Alpine skiing at Innsbruck, Austria. One of the first two U.S. athletes ever to win Olympic medals for skiing.

In 1970, he learned he had multiple sclerosis.

Although already concerned about recurrent problems with his eyes and coordination, Heuga was stunned.

"The morning before I was diagnosed, I ran five miles in under 25 minutes," Heuga says now. "And here was this doctor, getting all sad around the eyes, telling me I had MS. Hell, I was in better shape than he was."

By 1975, Heuga stumbled when he walked. He had stopped skiing, and, in accordance with doctors' advice, avoided most physical exertion. He was losing hope.

A desperate, last-ditch attempt to ride his bicycle one day ended in a crash—and a resolution. Refusing to accept confinement to a wheelchair, he started on a regimen of exercises to maintain his health and regain his coordination.

By 1977, he was skiing again. Biking. Swimming.

And since 1984, he has been helping others do the same, at the Jimmy Heuga Center for the Reanimation of the Physically Challenged, in Avon, Colo.

Says Heuga: "We want to maximize the quality of a person's health within the constraints of that person's condition."

Baltimore is back.

Once bustling, then battered, the Maryland seaport is back in business. Down and up is the story Baltimoreans tell about their city. Down began after World War II. The symptoms:

►Rising crime.
►A sinking harbor.
►Loss of manufacturing jobs.
►Population flight.

In the '60s and '70s, decaying and depopulated Baltimore was becoming a place to avoid.

Steve Weiner, 29, store manager, remembered Baltimore at the bottom: "Baltimore was picked on and looked over. It was just a place to pass through en route to or from New York. . . . Rats and bums were the only visitors to the harbor."

Rats, bums—and visionaries.

Not everyone had given up on the city. As early as the 1950s far-seeing mayors and planners envisioned a future for the central city. Even before the fall, the rebuilding began. One initiative followed another.

►Charles Center, established in 1958, 33 acres of skyscraping office towers in the heart of the business district.

►Inner Harbor, developed at the same time as Charles Center, a 207–acre waterfront complex of cultural and commercial establishments.

►Harborplace, opened in 1980, the hub of the Inner Harbor. A shopping and eating arcade developed by James Rouse, mastermind behind Boston's Quincy Market.

►The National Aquarium, opened in 1981, the crown jewel of the Inner Harbor.

More than 50 buildings later, the Charles Center-Inner Harbor complex has brought Baltimore's downtown back to vibrant, colorful, educational, entertaining life. Life shared by more than 18 million tourists each year.

Kyle Culpepper, 29, sportswear salesman and lifelong

Baltimore resident, described the current state of the city: "Now we're a national sightseeing place. We're more comparable to D.C. now. I think we're on the same scale as any big city."

But there's more to this city than visiting the aquarium. Problems remain in the residential areas. Crime. Chronic unemployment. Substandard housing. Poverty.

The downtown development hasn't solved everything, but it may have turned the tide. The light and life of the redeveloped area help the whole city in at least one obvious way. Image. Self-esteem.

Steve Weiner told us people had new respect for his city: "Baltimore is now on the map."

The details differ, but Baltimore's story is one we heard repeated often. The struggle of old cities to survive.

Some are further along in coping with the crime, unemployment and decay. Some have further to go. Problems and persistence are found at both ends of the spectrum.

►Pittsburgh. Jaws dropped and eyebrows rose when Rand McNally named this old steel town "America's Most Livable City" in 1986.

Pittsburgh had an image: Smoggy, smoky, ugly, depressed. The quintessential dying industrial city.

But facts can change faster than images.

The facts have been changing here ever since the 1950s when the city undertook the Renaissance project, a $500 million urban renewal program, which was followed up by Renaissance II, a $4.5 billion program launched in the late '70s.

Now sparkling, prosperous Pittsburgh has a new image. One that draws city planners from as far away as Japan.

Today's Pittsburgh: "It's a prototype city," says Kelly O'Toole, associate director of Greater Pittsburgh Office of Promotion. "Other cities are looking at us because we made the transition from a town that's dying to a town that's thriving."

►Camden, N.J., is not a success story.

New Jersey Gov. Tom Kean, 52, says straightforwardly, "Camden is a worst-case scenario."

Efforts have been expended but crime, decay and poverty have a heavy hold on the city.

But there is progress. From hopelessness to hopefulness. From impossible to possible.

Kean remembers the state of the city in 1982: ''When I campaigned in Camden, I literally almost cried.''

Other troubled cities, said the governor, had pockets of prosperity. Islands of activity. Not Camden.

''In Camden, there was nothing. I campaigned in Camden at a time when the mayor was on his way to jail. There wasn't anything under construction in the entire city. Not a house. Not an office.''

Now Camden is trying to catch up. Construction is under way on a $175 million waterfront park, which includes a $30 million aquarium along with office and retail space.

A familiar formula—but will it work? Too soon to tell. Too far to go before anyone can talk of a Camden renaissance. Not a success, but a beginning.

"Our Culture May Change, But It Will Continue"

Smiling, smocked Blue Corn, 66, doesn't look combative.

But the Pueblo Indian potter and mother of 10 is fighting a battle faced by many Native Americans. The struggle for cultural survival.

Though Blue Corn makes her pots the way her grandmother did, she says younger members of her pueblo in San Il Defonse, N.M., are less interested in continuing their culture.

''There are not many potters here,'' she told us. ''Because it's hard. Making a pot is not like turning on and off your radio.''

Modern culture, mass media and the job market all put pressure on Indians to be assimilated.

But Blue Corn has a solution.

She combines commerce and culture to lead a life that is both traditional and contemporary.

Her pots are known throughout the region, and among collectors across the country. She has been the subject of articles in *The Wall Street Journal* and *National Geographic*.

Her example has guided her daughter, Diane Calabaza, 30, who paints small pictures inspired by her tribe's religious dances and employing traditional images and symbols.

Not everyone can be a gifted potter. But we found Indians everywhere optimistically struggling to make their two worlds work together. United by a sense they have something to contribute.

Thelma Forrest, 47, Park Hill, Okla., manages a gift shop selling Indian crafts. Surrounds herself with Cherokee culture. But says that history and tradition don't have to be confining.

"I've read about the Trail of Tears, but I don't dwell on the past. Everybody has a history, some good and some bad. If there's something bad, you should try to fix it by looking to the future in a real positive way."

Forrest believes there is a way to combine the best of both cultures.

"Cherokees are moving into the mainstream. My two daughters went to college. Our culture may change, but it will continue. We can do anything."

"We Can't Live Our Lives in Fear"

Tami Graham, 40, Castle Rock, Wash., used to live in a two-story home on the banks of the Toutle River.

Moved out in a hurry May 18, 1980.

The day Mount St. Helens erupted.

The explosion:

▶Threw ash 13 miles into the air.

▶Triggered 100–mile-an-hour avalanches of burning rubble.

▶Decimated 150 square miles of forest.

▶Killed 57 people.

▶Destroyed Graham's house.

"It looked like a chocolate milkshake," she says of the bubbling mudslide that forced her family out of its house to the safety of higher ground.

Returning when the mud had settled and dried, the Grahams discovered the extent of the damage.

"When we walked out there on the crust of the mud, we saw that it had taken the top floor of our house downstream and left the main floor full of mud. We lost all of our possessions. I cried for four days."

Seven years after the eruption, the Grahams have a new house. Trees planted in the ash have grown to 10 to 12 feet. Animals have reappeared.

The mountain is still there, still dangerous, but the Grahams are determined to lead normal lives.

"For two years, I paid attention to the rumblings and false alarms. But we, along with a lot of others in this community, feel like we have to go on with our lives. I can't live my life in fear."

Survivors Across the USA

There ain't no work here. The out-of-state companies bring people with them. The big coal companies buy up everything and put regulations this way and that way. The little man doesn't have a chance.

BOBBY MITCHELL

Few face a challenge as menacing as Mount St. Helens. But day to day, and coast to coast, we all face problems. And many of us face them with an impressive amount of perseverance and optimism.

▶Bobby Mitchell, 28, Walton, Ky., faces the most common challenge of them all. Unemployment.

"There ain't no work here. The out-of-state companies bring people with them. The big coal companies buy up everything and put regulations this way and that way. The little man doesn't have a chance."

But Mitchell's rural residence and raising give him resources to get by, he says. "I can live with or without working. I live on a farm, grow my own food. Do odds-and-ends jobs. There's no work, but it's pretty."

▶Terry McKusky, 33, coordinator at the Iron Gate Shopping Mall, in Hibbing, Minn., says the people of Minnesota's depressed Iron Range are tough enough to survive the current hard times. Committed to continuing their communities and way of life. "Iron Rangers are survivors. People are looking at the real possibilities that their jobs may go. They are loyal to this area. I lived in Minneapolis for seven years, but I came back. Once an Iron Ranger, always an Iron Ranger.''

▶Renee Miller, 25, motel clerk, Mountain Home, Idaho, is a single parent on a shoestring. Says a depressed economy is no reason for a depressed outlook: ''This town has military people, retired military people and people on welfare. Once you get a job, you don't let go of it. I make $3.35 an hour, and I'm glad to get it. We're making it. We pay our bills and have fun.''

▶The USA is a nation of survivors.

Adversity is said to test character, and wherever we found adversity we found an abundance of character:

▶Flexibility and smarts on the farm.

▶Optimism in the oil field.

▶Courage and compassion among the challenged and sick.

▶Strength and spirit among the unemployed, impoverished.

Of course, there are other emotions and reactions. Anger. Frustration. Despair.

But across a range of backgrounds and situations, most of the people most of the time look for the good in the bad. Hope and opportunity.

Meet trouble with tenacity.

Survive through thick and thin. And search for ways to thrive.

7 GIVING IS PART OF LIVING

Charity is reaching beyond our back yards. We're contributing money and time to worthy causes. Caring and sharing have taken on a new dimension. Volunteerism is in vogue.

HELPING HANDS: Betty Dulaney helps Sally Jones review reading and writing skills in Tunica, Miss.

he BusCapade was only an hour old. We'd just parked on a street corner next to the county courthouse in Potosi, Mo.

Marilyn Bust, red-headed former Miss Potosi, pulled up in the middle of North Missouri Street and called us over to her car.

"Happy St. Patrick's Day," smiled the 66–year-old homemaker as she handed us a plate of corned beef sandwiches.

Within the next two hours:

►Ted Kelderman, 48, and his wife, Beverley, 48, who own the Dutch Dairy, brought us St. Patrick-green crushed-ice cones.

►Banker Harold Turner, 56, took us to the historic former Church of God, now remodeled to house his bank, and gave us souvenir pens and yardsticks.

►Neil Richards, 48, who, with his 78–year-old mother, Ruby, runs *The* (Potosi) *Independent-Journal,* gave us a book commemorating Potosi's 1963 bicentennial.

From Anchorage to Albany, from Woonsocket, R.I., to Walla Walla, Wash., there is a spirit of sharing and caring all across the USA. The spirit did not surprise us. The scope of the giving did.

►Dollars and doughnuts.
►Bales of hay and bundles of baby clothes.
►Day-care centers and summer camps.
►Time and toil.

In 1986, charitable contributions in the USA totaled a record $87.2 billion, an increase of 9.4 percent over 1985. Mainly from individuals. But corporations are also active. The USA's largest corporations make charitable contributions totaling billions of dollars.

The people of the USA give their time as well as their money. About 48 percent of all adults and 52 percent of teen-agers volunteer. Value: an estimated $100 billion worth of time. Twenty-three million give five or more hours of their time each week.

The time and dollars add up. To hope. To dreams. To opportunity.

"I Just Thank God the School Is There"

To some, Tunica, Miss., may seem like a county with a broken heart. But it has heart.

Traveling for weeks, stopping for hours, we sometimes found that cities and towns blurred together. Malls, McDonald's and middle-class mildness sometimes obscured a city's unique character.

Not Tunica. There is no mall in Tunica. There isn't even a supermarket.

Despite rich land for farming, Tunica is the poorest county in the poorest state in the USA.

▶Unemployment of almost 18 percent.

▶Average per capita income of about $4,000.

▶Virtually no industry, with a handful of small factories providing only about 400 jobs.

The atmosphere here is different. Hotter, slower, sadder.

This town has known hard times for so long it seems more resigned than distressed. Idle men rest on downtown benches; the little daytime traffic consists mainly of rumbling, rusty relics.

But not everyone accepts the status quo.

There may be poverty and pessimism in some quarters, but there is also pride and potential.

Greeting the BusCapade that warm day in April was Betty Jo Dulaney, a woman with a plan.

"I've always volunteered for things. It's the way I was brought up," says Dulaney, 47. When she learned that Tunica County had the highest rate of illiteracy in Mississippi, she volunteered to help.

"We have people who don't even know their ABCs. They're starting from step one. My goal is to take them up to the ninth-grade reading level. From there they can go on to earn their high school graduation equivalency degree."

Working with federal programs to buy books and plan a course of study, Dulaney organized an attack on Tunica's adult illiteracy.

Although previous attempts attracted few students,

Dulaney found 31 for her first class. Eight months later she had 10 "completers"—students who had mastered the two skill books at the heart of the program. Just one dropout. She attributes her success at finding students to a little common sense and a lot of legwork.

"You have to go where the students are. That's what I've done. I've gone to the black community. I've been to the churches. I've been to the welfare department. I've been to the laundromat."

Those efforts started a cycle that seems to be self-perpetuating—students are now bringing friends and family members.

Sally Jones, 67, enrolled in the program to continue an education that ended in the fifth grade over half a century ago. Although she can read "pretty good" and write cursive, Jones wanted to learn how to print.

"When my kids write to me, they like to print," says Jones. "I think it looks pretty, and I wanted to learn how to do it."

Going back to school means classes twice a week and homework in between. Jones is happy to do the work.

"I always have a piece of paper around to practice on. I've always wanted to further my education. I just thank God the school is there."

While buoyed by students' gratitude and feelings of accomplishment, Dulaney says much remains to be done.

"If I read my statistics right," she says, "there are about 3,212 people in this community who could benefit from our program."

That's a big order, but Dulaney is encouraged by the successes so far. Already two formerly unemployed students have completed the program and found full-time jobs.

"That's what this program is all about. Getting people up on their own two feet."

A Real-Life Home on the Range

While Betty Jo Dulaney's students and volunteers pore over workbooks in the Mississippi delta, another group of students 2,000 miles away on the Nebraska plains is learning other, even more essential skills: how to live without hurting themselves or others, how to love.

Having seen *Boys Town*, the movie, we were eager to visit Boys Town, the institution.

Ten miles west of Omaha, we found the statue of a teen-ager carrying a younger boy on his shoulders.

The inscription: "He ain't heavy, Father . . . he's my brother." We knew we were in the right place.

Father Edward Flanagan, the spectacled, thoughtful founder of Boys Town, did not set out to become a household name or a symbol of our potential for good. He set out to help troubled young men. Hollywood and Spencer Tracy took care of the rest.

The community that began as Father Flanagan's Boys Home in 1917, in a rented house with 90 borrowed dollars, is now a bustling, busy community with 500 young people in residence.

Young people, not boys: 20 percent of the residents are female. Boys Town has been admitting girls since 1979.

Boys Town has changed in other ways, too. The scope of its activities has grown to include The Boys Town National Institute, a speech and hearing hospital that has treated more than 5,300 children free of charge, and spin-off mini-campuses such as Boys Town of Central Florida.

Despite these changes, sentimental movie fans would still recognize it. The community's trademarks endure:

►Residents still govern themselves, electing a mayor from among the students.

►There is still the air of respect and trust that made Father Flanagan's experiment so novel in 1917.

Father Val Peter, 53, the current executive director, told us Boys Town's purpose remains what it was under Father Flanagan. "When a boy or girl comes here he is filled with pain and hurt. He wonders if there is such a thing as hope, a second chance. He wonders if there really is a place where he can open his heart just a little bit. Boys Town is that place."

The students range in age from 9 to 18; average stay is 18 months.

Many are referred by social workers, some simply

show up after seeing the movie. Such walk-ons are called "pilgrims" and are never turned away.

The average Boys Town resident has lived in four foster homes; most are two or three years behind in their reading and writing.

"We take kids everybody's given up on," says Father Peter. "We keep them safe from abuse and neglect. We help them. We teach skills that can be repeated through life. And most importantly, we make a person happy."

For most of Boys Town's students, happiness has been scarce indeed. Gathered around a summer campfire, one girl told Father Peter she liked Boys Town simply because it was safe. When he asked her what she meant, she said she no longer had to worry when she went to bed that someone would bother her during the night.

It puzzled him that a girl who had been hurt by those she trusted could learn to trust again. Father Peter asked her how she knew she was safe.

Her answer: "She said that even though he was dead, she knew that Father Flanagan was up in heaven looking down, and that he wouldn't let anything bad happen to her."

The girl also thought Father Peter stayed awake all night, driving around the school to make sure all was well.

Says Father Peter, "She had both heaven and earth on her side. I'd say that's a pretty secure feeling."

In addition to giving students emotional support, Boys Town focuses on teaching them the skills and habits essential to success in life and work.

Todd Shoup, 16, told us he has lived in Boys Town four years.

"My probation officer suggested I come here. She said this was my last chance or I would be sent upstate to a lockup.

"My family-teachers have taught me a lot. Social skills like greeting somebody, holding a conversation, being able to follow instructions and accepting criticism. There are so many advantages here it's amazing."

The bonds formed at Boys Town often endure long after leaving. Almost one-third of the 16,000 alumni are actively involved with the school.

Alumni also contribute to the 40 percent of Boys Town's annual budget funded by public donations. Another 40 percent is furnished by interest from the Boys Town Foundation, established by Father Flanagan in 1941. Twenty percent comes as reimbursement for services from government agencies.

"Our alumni feel that Boys Town is their home," says Father Peter. "They come back to Boys Town just like any boy goes home. They don't have to have a reason."

For generations of young men and a generation of young women, this famous place has been a place of shelter and security on the harsh Nebraska plains. A real-life home on the range.

We asked Father Peter about the impact of the seemingly monotonous Nebraska landscape on his students.

"I think it's very symbolic that Boys Town is on the great Nebraska Prairie. The prairie is symbolic of freedom, the ability to roam as you want, free as a bird. It's a glorious feeling. The prairie teaches a lesson of courage, compassion.

"Any dope can look at the seashore and be inspired because it shouts at you. So do the mountains. But the prairie only whispers. You must listen closely and never miss the message."

Listening to whispers in the hearts of troubled youths, seeing the beauty others overlook, Father Peter and the staff of Boys Town go about their work day in and day out, decades after the movie has left the theaters.

Perhaps it's time for a sequel.

A Charitable Hustler

Summer camp was on Paul Newman's mind as the BusCapade wound its way through Connecticut. Not just any summer camp, but the free summer camp for critically ill children that Newman and his partners are building on 300 acres in rural northeastern Connecticut.

The Hole in the Wall Gang Camp—named after the band of bad guys in *Butch Cassidy and the Sundance Kid*—is being built to resemble a turn-of-the-century mining camp. Log cabins, horses, even a "saloon." The dispensary and medical staff will be as unobtrusive as possible.

For the 500 children ages 7 to 17 who will spend two summer weeks here, it will be a change of pace and place from the hospitals and clinics that are the ordinary regimen of illness.

"I have lost some friends in midlife," Newman told us. "And I thought how fortunate they were to at least have a sense of accomplishment for the life they had. And I wondered about the children. It seemed if we could give children a few weeks of camping experience outside of a hospital, it would be a real accomplishment."

To finance the venture, the star of *The Sting, The Hustler* and *The Color of Money* has done what some of his most memorable characters did best: He hustled.

Five years ago, Newman teamed up with longtime friend and business associate A.E. Hotchner to manufacture and market food products, starting with a salad dressing, that would trade off of Newman's celebrity.

The brand would be called "Newman's Own."

His famous name would appear on every package. His famous face would appear on every label. His famous blue eyes would stare out at each contemplating consumer.

Fast Eddie Felsen would have been proud—until he found out they were giving away the money.

Five years later, Newman's Own line has grown to include spaghetti sauce, popcorn, lemonade.

The company's charitable contributions have totaled more than $13 million. The money has gone to charities ranging from Ethiopian famine relief to The New York Times' Neediest Cases fund.

The Paul Newman food empire produces food in factories from Toronto to Australia, but corporate headquarters are still furnished with a pingpong table and lounge chairs from Newman's swimming pool.

The summer camp is the company's crowning achievement and the cause nearest to its founders' hearts.

As Newman makes clear, it is a vast cooperative effort, made possible by the contributions and sacrifices of thousands from all walks of life, from the Yale University doctors designing the medical facilities to the $5 million contribution from Saudi Arabia's King Fahd.

But the vision and the spirit that made it happen—like the salad dressing and the Industrial Strength Venetian Spaghetti Sauce—are Newman's Own.

"Their Work Ethic Rubs Off"

Joan Pearson Kelly, 59, of Bellefontaine, Ohio, gives on a more personal scale.

The bright-eyed, silver-haired housewife gives her time, and her tea, to make her town a warmer place for a few of the many Japanese women moving into the area.

A central location, a highly qualified workforce and the availability of raw materials have all contributed to the proliferation of Japanese factories in central Ohio as elsewhere in the Midwest in recent years.

Thanks to her Culture Club, Kelly has, too.

While others focused on economics and politics, Kelly was propelled by sympathy for Japanese families facing the demands of a new country, language and culture.

She was especially sympathetic to the women, who faced much of the grind of relocation—packing, unpacking, finding the right shops and reliable doctors for the children—and who often faced it alone while their husbands worked.

To help out, Kelly organized her Culture Club. Weekly meetings with a small group of Japanese women make them feel at home and let them practice their English.

And now, she says, the giving goes both ways.

"We eat their raw fish. I like it. They teach us about Japanese holidays like Girls Day and Boys Day.

"Their work ethic rubs off. They've made more Ohioans willing to work all day Saturday or late at night."

Sharing and caring may be old, eternal human ideas. But that doesn't mean they can't be improved.

In earlier times, charity necessarily began at home. Friends and family were usually nearby and neighbors lifelong. If one member of a community faced hardship, others knew about it and took action.

While this pattern endures, increasing mobility and reliance on mass media have altered our way of giving. Our mobility makes us less likely to know the person—and the needs—down the street or across the hall. Yet our access to modern communications helps to make neighbors out of earthquake victims or famine sufferers half a world away.

We don't hear about someone's trouble on the grapevine. We see it on the evening news.

Of course, the power of television has not been overlooked by those seeking to raise funds.

The dramatic growth of telethons is testament that a worthy cause and a bank of telephones can turn a modest effort into a megacharity.

Case in point: Jerry Lewis' Labor Day Telethon for Muscular Dystrophy. The most recent edition of the telethon raised a record $39.021 million, surpassing the previous year's record by almost $5 million.

Beginning with a single television station in 1966, the telethon is now carried by close to 200 stations.

Over the course of 22 years, Lewis has raised more than $404,000,000.

Although the growing competition among telethons and the escalating costs of televising them have combined to put the future of some telethons in doubt, new and different ways of using television are always being devised.

▶Rock bands fought world hunger with a Live Aid concert.

▶Country music performers reached out to the heartland with cablecasts of their Farm Aid concerts.

▶On HBO, comedians told jokes and raised funds on Comic Relief.

Most of us have wondered at times if charity is a thing of the past. A cherished holdover, continuing in quiet corners, but crushed in the big cities by the pressure and pace.

BusCapade found a different picture.

Bigger and busier, the cities and suburbs are not necessarily less caring than old-fashioned small towns. Modern life can make charity challenging, but the mainstream is not so far from Main Street.

Not everyone can make the contributions of a Father Flanagan or a Paul Newman. But millions more do what they can.

Riding the roads through small towns and big cities, we saw people in all walks of life doing their share of sharing. The causes and charities vary, and so do the amount and nature of our support, but most folks try to make some sort of contribution to their communities.

From college students to retirees.

►Paul Raynis, 21, a graduate student at the University of Missouri, came to a late-night bull session to tell us rumors of his generation's selfishness were greatly exaggerated. Contributing doesn't have to mean joining the Peace Corps, he says. "I want to make a hell of a lot of money but I want to spend it on some liberal causes. How do you define me?"

►Bill Swigart, 65, Salem, Ore., volunteers 20 hours each week at the local library. He says it beats watching television. "I even got a raise this year: I get twice as many cookies."

►Mike Smith, 21, of Shelbyville, Ky., was eating lunch at Ralph's Market when we talked to him. He had worked up the appetite for a two-Ralphburger lunch while helping his neighbor clean up and rebuild after a fire that destroyed his mill. Embers still smoldered as they went about clearing the ground for a new building. Lunch was Smith's only payment, and that he accepted reluctantly.

►In Newark, N.J., a troubled city that seems to be coming back, we met Jim Keyes, 26, who believes in taking responsibility for the safety of his community.

"Every town has its good sections and its bad sections. If you live in a bad section it's your duty to clean it up," says Keyes. "We have block associations. I'm not going to allow crime to go on on my block."

▶Many help by contributing to organizations like the American Red Cross, the United Way and UNICEF—the IBMs and GMs of charity. The big ones employ thousands, use sophisticated demographic analyses to solicit contributions and operate on a national or international scale. But they are in the same business.

William Aramony, 60, president of United Way of America, described the impact of that organization. "Every level of society participates. The United Way system of payroll giving allows everybody to be a philanthropist. We've democratized philanthropy."

Large charities share another characteristic with smaller efforts: their dependence on the generosity of the USA.

Although he has headed the United Way for 17 years, Aramony is still staggered by our willingness to share. "The generosity of Americans' support of philanthropic activities is beyond measure. The USA is the premier country in not only the amount, but in the variety and the commitment to voluntary giving and philanthropy. We really believe in it. It's incredible."

We saw that kind of commitment all along the highways and byways of the USA. Caring and compassion continue. Giving is very much a part of living across the USA.

Every town has its good sections. If you live in a bad section it's your duty to clean it up. We have block associations. I'm not going to allow crime to go on on my block.

JIM KEYES

8 KEEPING THE FAITH

Faith is a full-time commitment for many of us. Even the distance between denominations has lessened as different religions work to unite us.

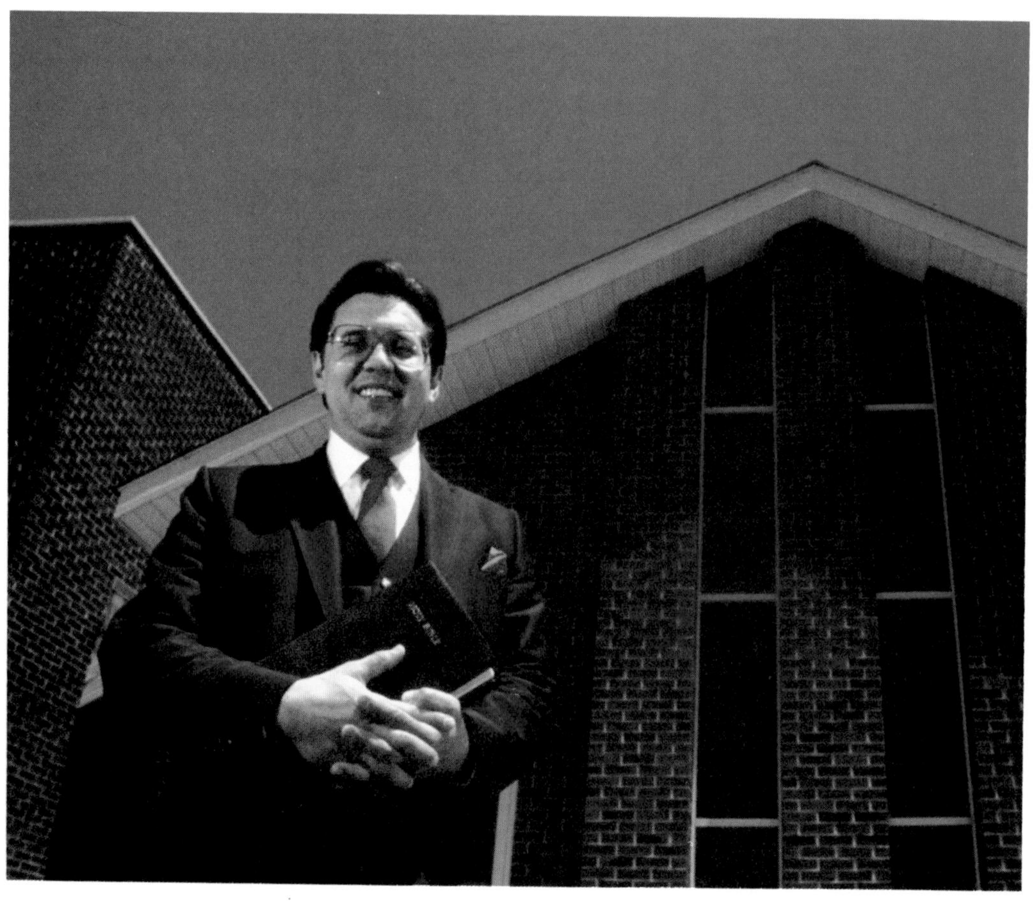

FOCUS ON FAITH: The Rev. Edwin Harper, pastor of the Apostolic Church in Huntington, W.Va., says "churchianity" is big in West Virginia.

he three Rs are very much a part of our weekend lifestyle:

▶Religion.
▶Rest.
▶Recreation.

Despite competition from the latter two, old-fashioned churchgoing is still second nature on Sunday for many of us.

According to a USA TODAY survey:

▶44 percent say they attend church weekly.

▶16 percent say they attend a few times a month.

▶31 percent say they go to church occasionally or rarely.

▶9 percent say they never go.

And that's just part of the story.

While churches and temples may be fitting forums to discuss religion, people are more important than steeples. And the religious feelings of people in the USA clearly are not confined to churches. Or to Sundays.

In a country where the currency declares "In God We Trust" and religious programs are as close as the cable television selector, faith for many is a full-time commitment.

A recent poll found 95 percent of people in the USA believe in God. On our tour, we found that faith almost everywhere:

▶Among Mormons and miners.
▶From ministers to mechanics.
▶Shared by televangelists and traffic clerks.
▶From cathedrals to convenience stores.

For people across the USA, from all walks of life, faith is the foundation for the way they live and the way they work. Seven days a week.

"Churchianity"

"The hardest thing to find in West Virginia is someone who admits to being a sinner," says the Rev. Edwin S.

Harper, pastor of the Apostolic Church in Huntington. "I believe the national average is taken on Easter Sunday. I'd say 42 percent of the people in West Virginia attend church regularly.

"The boys and girls of West Virginia may leave the state and broaden their horizons, but they still feel it's hard to violate the 'churchianity' they learned almost from birth in West Virginia."

That "churchianity" loomed large in our conversations with West Virginians. Mentions of faith came frequently and comfortably.

Sharon Gresham, 29, a personnel specialist from South Charleston, told us churches play a big role in a person's identity.

"The first question most people I meet ask is what church I belong to," she said.

With unemployment topping 9 percent, West Virginia is not the easiest place to make a living. And many of the existing jobs can be dirty and dangerous.

"The harshness of life makes religion a serious thing," says the Rev. Charles Echols, 44, of the United Methodist Church in Huntington. "If you're a coal miner and you might die this afternoon, you want to be sure God is there."

The Mormon Majority

Halfway across the nation, there's another state where faith is foremost for many.

The Utah-based Church of Jesus Christ of Latter-day Saints—better known as the Mormons—is a church of:

▶6.1 million adherents worldwide.

▶1,241,000 members in Utah. 73 percent of the state's population.

▶Many, even most, prominent figures in Utah.

▶Strong stands on matters of morals. Industry and abstinence—from alcohol, smoking, caffeine, non-marital sex—are important elements of Mormon culture.

And of Utah's culture: Not only do Mormons have strong ideas about morality, here they have the power to make them law. Stricter-than-average laws to restrict the sale of alcohol are one consequence of that power.

Majority rule is the essence of democracy. And in Utah, the majority is Mormon.

In no other state were questions about the separation of church and state raised so regularly.

Utah Gov. Norman Bangerter, 54, a Mormon: "That's always a topic of discussion with this being the headquarters of the Mormon Church. Obviously, you tend to reflect your upbringing and the culture in which you reside. Certainly, the church doesn't come in and say 'You will do this,' or 'You won't do that.' "

David Adcock, 40, disagrees. We met this former Mormon drinking a beer in a bar in Ogden. Protesting the power of Mormon morality.

"The Mormons took my library away from me—they took the *Penthouses* and *Playboys* out of the 7-Elevens. I bought a satellite dish to watch the Playboy channel. I like to have the option of making a choice for myself."

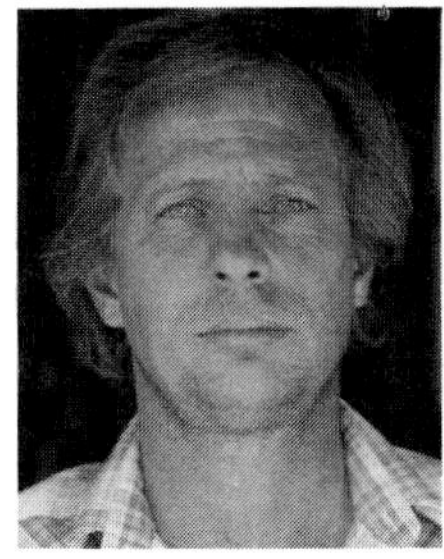

The Mormons took my library away from me—they took the Penthouses *and* Playboys *out of the 7-Elevens. . . . I like to have the option of making a choice for myself.*
DAVID ADCOCK

Shauna Peterson, 18, Mormon, maintains that Utahans do have the option to choose for themselves. And they choose to follow the church's teaching.

"I don't need to get drunk to have fun. I think hanging around in malls or driving up and down the street in a car would be boring. I won't go to see an R-rated movie because I disapprove of all the sex in them. That's what my family has taught me, and it's my decision, too."

The Spiritual Water Slide

By the time we pulled into Heritage USA in Fort Mill, S.C., we half expected to find an amusement park populated entirely by bill collectors. After all, during the preceding months, this Christian theme park had had its share of troubles:

▶Founder Jim Bakker had to step down after admitting a sexual encounter with former church secretary Jessica Hahn.

▶New PTL chairman Jerry Falwell was pleading for contributions simply to meet payroll.

▶The park teetered at the edge of bankruptcy, with debts totaling $68 million.

Surely, we couldn't blame these people if they were a little disheartened and depressed.

They were anything but. They had all the joy and exuberance of middle-age Mouseketeers. And clearly, these people had found something more important in their lives than Annette.

"Heritage USA is a re-firing center for Christians from all over the country to come to relax and still be in a Christian atmosphere," says Don Hardister Jr., 36, vice president of PTL.

"Everything here has a spiritual emphasis. There's a spiritual emphasis in the jewelry store. There's a spiritual emphasis on the water park, on the water slide."

There's even a spiritual emphasis in Tammy Faye Bakker's Cosmetics store.

Millie Freeman, 51, a sales clerk and good friend of Tammy Faye, explains how her face reflects her faith: "We want to stay beautiful for the Lord. I don't think the Lord wants you to look haggard. He wants you to look nice."

Although Heritage USA may sometimes be on shaky ground, the visitors we met at the park were firm in their faith.

"Almost anywhere you go in South Carolina, there's a deep-roots feeling about Christianity," says Chuck Martin, a real estate consultant from Fort Mill. "More people are coming into the church. More people are getting saved."

"I Believe He Heard"

Jim and Tammy Faye Bakker weren't the only evangelists in the news.

When Oral Roberts announced that God had told him he must raise $8 million or die, skeptics abounded. But in Tulsa, Okla., home of Oral Roberts University, support stayed strong.

Faith works in mysterious ways, people here told us.

But it does work. Many cited Roberts' accomplishments here as proof of the power.

Already prayer and preaching, broadcasting and fund-raising had built a massive, modern education and health complex on the outskirts of Tulsa:

►A 4,500–student university.
►A $500 million campus.
►A spindle-shaped prayer tower soaring 100 feet in the sky.
►The City of Faith Health Care Center, aimed at merging modern medicine with healing prayer. Among its facilities:
►A 60–story diagnostic clinic.
►A 30–story hospital.
►A 20–story research center.

"Expect a miracle," Roberts exhorts his followers, in person and on his long-running television program. And so they did.

While much of the country gossiped and stared and counted the days as the preacher's April deadline approached, Roberts and his followers prayed. Waited for something to happen.

And then something did happen: Jerry Collins, a Florida race track entrepreneur, stepped forward with a $1.3 million check that put Roberts over his goal.

Four months later, when we arrived on campus, the controversy was cooling, but Dean Dew, 31, a junior majoring in business, was eager to give his perspective:

"People took a lot of what he said and misquoted him. He really feels God is calling him to do God's will. God spoke to him. I believe a man can hear from God and I believe he heard."

Faith carried the school through the crisis, said Dew. The same faith that carries the school in all of its activities: "This isn't heaven, but it's the closest I've found."

Carolyn Smith, 24, a research technician at the university medical school, agreed. She recalled how faith played a role in her eye surgery: "The surgeon gathered my family together and prayed with us. . . . That meant so much because the surgeon, who is a skilled and talented man, still knew who was guiding his hands."

For some on campus, faith brings comfort. For others, it also brings confidence. And for some, it brings line drives and grounders.

Chad Fields, 19, a first baseman on the Oral Roberts baseball team, says, "I know that God gave me my ability to play baseball. I pray that the ball will be hit to me every time."

Pilgrimage

BusCapade reached Miami one week ahead of Pope John Paul II.

Florida's largest metropolitan area was one of the last stops on our journey. It was also the first stop on a 10-city tour of the USA by the Roman Catholic pontiff.

Roaming Miami a week before the pope's arrival, BusCapade found the level of excitement high and climbing.

▶Billboards welcoming the pontiff.

▶Ribbons of yellow and white—the papal colors—tied to trees and car antennas.

▶An oversized string of rosary beads draped around a downtown skyscraper.

The pope is even more important than the president. He's our spiritual leader.
ELIZABETH CANDELARIA

Elizabeth Candelaria, 25, a passport photographer in Miami Beach, told of her plans for the approaching event: "When the pope comes I'm going to take out my biggest lenses and climb up on somebody's roof."

Her reason: "The pope is even more important than the president. He's our spiritual leader."

Keeping the Faith Across the USA

From Miami to Maine, from athletes to academics, we heard echoes of Candelaria's faith in a higher power. Some of the other faces of faith:

▶Rabbi Laszlo Berkowits, 61, Falls Church, Va. Tapped his fingers on his lips as he thought through his remarks. "Faith infuses life with transcendent meaning," he told us. "Life isn't just two plus two."

Rabbi Berkowits told us of his interaction with the clergy of the other faiths. Said they faced the same problems. Addressed the same universal human needs: "Religions in this country more than get along. We are working together."

►E. J. Johnson, 43, mechanic, Clarksdale, Miss.: "I used to be into the blues, but now I sing spiritual. We have a group called the Gospel Soul Singers. We don't sing for money. We sing for the gospel, to praise the Lord."

►Kathy Hanna, 24, saleswoman at LeRoy's Jewelry, Charleston, W.Va.: "We were raised going to church and Sunday school every week. I don't go now because I have to work on Sundays. When I have kids, they'll have to go to Sunday school. I went, and I turned out OK."

►Lequetta "Cricket" Stone, 32, florist, Topeka, Kan.: "I grew up on a farm. Farmers make their living off of what God provides them. They're not greedy. They're thankful for what they have rather than stuck on what they don't have or could have."

►Roger Anderson, 56, machinist, Bremerton, Wash., visiting Yellowstone National Park in Wyoming: "You wonder what the first mountain men thought when they saw this land. I wish I had been here when they opened up the land, with game all over the place. People say things were created by evolution, but this place makes you think again. This couldn't just happen. It has to be God's work."

►Father Joseph Hayden, 50, a Catholic priest in Springfield, Ky. Grew up 10 miles from the congregation he now heads. Calls that a helpful background in that conservative area: "I knew the way they'd always done it here. And I kept it that way."

Says devotion runs deeper than a love of tradition: "Kentucky's greatest asset is a strong faith. It gives them a purpose in life. A meaning. They can keep going no matter what happens."

Faith.

Hard to measure, hard to define. Hard to overlook.

Some call our society secular, many believe religion to be in decline. But across the USA, our conversations came time after time to God.

From rabbis and reverends to soldiers and scientists, most of the people we met included a religious element when describing what was most meaningful to them.

Like every aspect of society, religion has changed in recent years. Some see a decline in devotion, others a broadening definition. But two things are clear:

▶The distance between denominations has lessened. Differences of doctrine endure, but distrust and fear have waned. Mutual respect has grown.

▶Faith flourishes. Whether in an institutional affiliation, or a personal philosophy. Not everyone believes the same things, or believes with the same intensity, but faith is a force in most of our lives.

9 A NATION ON VACATION

We value our vacations. They're
a chance to focus on the
fantasy of a stress-free lifestyle.

SALMON SEASON: Oil worker Jerry Stinson doesn't seem to mind the crowded, chaotic, peak fishing season on Alaska's Russian River that some have called "combat fishing."

ome interviews were more strenuous than others.

In Eugene, Ore., our reporters came back to the bus a little short of breath after on-the-run interviews with several of the city's joggers.

Kathi Wiederhold, 32, out running with a co-worker, showed us mercy. She stopped.

"We run on our break and eat at our desk after lunch," said Wiederhold, a land-use planner. "We talk about lunch while we jog and what we're going to eat when we stop."

Running nearby were Sandra Huffstutter, 38, and her husband, Allen, 39. They told us the only time they see each other is when they run together.

"We're a two-career family with two teen-age sons and a big house to take care of," explained Sandra. The Huffstutters, married for 18 years, alternate three-mile jogs with aerobic workouts.

We saw that kind of lifestyle all across the USA.

Whether running or roller skating, canoeing or camping, reading or rehearsing for an amateur orchestra—this is a nation that values recreation.

More and more mini-vacations, for a few hours, or a weekend, or a few days, supplement our traditional two weeks of vacation. Leisure consumes an ever-increasing amount of our time and money:

▶Camping: Sightseers paid 344 million visits to national parks in 1985. Up from 172 million in 1970.

▶Bowling: 67 million bowled in 1985. An increase from 52 million in 1970.

▶Reading: Sales of books and maps in 1985 totaled almost 8 billion. Compared with 3 billion in 1970.

From Florida's beaches to Colorado's ski slopes, to Minnesota's 10,000 lakes to Arizona's deserts, people across the USA work hard at playing.

A Fantasy Town

In Aspen, Colo., leisure is a way of life.

A century-old mining town turned worldclass ski resort, Aspen is both rustic and refined. Most of all, relaxed.

Aspen is a fantasy town. The cops wear shorts and drive around in Saabs. Money is the focus here. People come to see how much pleasure they can buy.

AARON BOCKSTEDT

Or tries to be. Locals here told tales of "power shoppers" and described their town as a "taxi stand for Lear jets." Some said social competition and conspicuous consumption eclipse genuine recreation.

But that may be oversimplifying. In Aspen, the most exclusive enclave of an upscale sport, spending money is part of the fun.

And Aspen's inhabitants are clearly getting something in return for their cash. A few of the assets in Aspen's portfolio:

- ►80 restaurants.
- ►More than 200 retail shops.
- ►3,243 acres of ski slopes.
- ►A free system of public transportation.
- ►An abundance of the arts. Including a repertory theater, a ballet company and a summertime music festival.
- ►All this in a town with just 5,000 year-round residents.

The bottom line is a stress-free lifestyle of luxury and convenience, winter and summer. Snow and skiing give way to hiking and open-air theater. Residents told us the skiing brought them here and the summers make them stay.

The best perspective may come from those who live and work here year-round.

Aaron Bockstedt, 20, a convenience store clerk, complained about the cost of living. Said he has trouble affording the staples he sells. Noted that most here don't have that problem:

"Aspen is a fantasy town. The cops wear shorts and drive around in Saabs. Money is the focus here. People come to see how much pleasure they can buy."

Easygoing Ray Metz, 42, may epitomize Aspen. Smiling and prosperous behind pricey sunglasses, he told us how he came to settle here, and of the life he has made:

"I sold my company eight years ago and moved to Aspen. I came here to relax, not to read the out-of-state newspapers.

"I drive a bus so I can ski for free. It's like college:

Everybody here does odd jobs. I know a dentist who does ski patrol during the winter. It's a grown-up Disneyland. Life in Aspen is a movie.''

"Combat Fishing"

We met plenty of folks who truly enjoy the Great Outdoors. Some take their vacations in the nation's woodlands; others take weekend hunting and fishing trips. But for the truly serious sportsman and sportswoman, there's the ultimate option: Move to Alaska.

On a cool, drizzly day in June, we stood on the banks of the Russian River, watching fishermen stand shoulder-to-shoulder, knee-deep in the frigid water, pulling in hundreds of salmon.

During the summer, at the peak of the season, the fishing waters can become crowded with flailing fishing poles. The resulting chaos—and the occasional hooked fishermen—led one writer to describe the scene as ''combat fishing.''

But the crowds didn't seem to disturb Jerry Stinson, 33, as he proudly displayed his catch. ''In the Lower 48, you're lucky to catch a minnow,'' said the oil worker from Soldotna, Alaska. ''Here I hooked and landed seven kings (salmon), the biggest at 40 pounds. It is the last frontier.''

Fishing nearby was Judy Tankersley, 30, of Anchorage. ''I caught a 35–pound king,'' she said. ''It gave me a 20–minute fight. I usually bake them or send them to my family in Reno.''

Of course, Alaska has challenges as well as charms: Wide expanses of rugged terrain. Severe weather. A boom-or-bust economy.

And then there's the matter of day and night. Daylight shrinks to three hours and 42 minutes at the winter solstice. Darkness lasts 21 hours and 18 minutes.

While winters can be daunting, many take full advantage of the extra hours of daylight during the summer.

''In the summertime, it's like working in vacationland,'' says Ed Unger, 27, an oil drilling engineer from

Anchorage. "After I get off, I've still got eight hours of sunlight. I play in golf tournaments where we tee off at 12 midnight."

Taking a Chance

Wading knee-deep in a rushing river isn't enough of an adventure for many in the USA. These brave souls take their chances in a casino.

Gambling is a prime source of recreation in this country, but it's also big business. Nowhere bigger than in Las Vegas:

- ▶52 major hotel-casinos.
- ▶58,500 guest rooms.
- ▶Eight of the 10 biggest hotels in the world.
- ▶$8 billion annual revenues from the tourism industry.

Vegas. City of stretch limousines and long-legged chorus girls. Big-name entertainers. Home of the world's largest neon sign. The gambling center of the USA. Maybe the world.

You can golf, hunt, hike or swim here. You can see a show or catch a comedian. You can dine in five languages. Or you can simply lounge in the luxury of a $1,200 duplex suite.

But that isn't why you come to Vegas.

You come to Vegas for blackjack. Poker. Roulette. Baccarat. Craps. Keno. Slot machines—58,000 of them.

The Vegas stakes:

- ▶$2.7 billion was won and lost here in 1987.
- ▶$163 million in profits was banked by the casinos.

Gambling brought this city into being. Gambling made the desert sprout skyscrapers. Gambling brings the planeloads of tourists. Pays the rents and salaries. Fuels the economy and lights the signs. Defines the city and its style.

But not everyone here gambles. Long-term Vegas residents told us that a steady paycheck may be the best bet in town.

Robin Dorand, 38, makes her living as a pit boss. Told a familiar story: "When I first came to Las Vegas I was having an affair with a 25–cent slot machine that lived at the Riviera. One day it ate my whole paycheck of $160. That was the rent, the food money and the car payments. I literally cried. Ever since then I rarely play."

Vegas may be the biggest and the best-known. But it is no longer the only. From lotteries to legalized casinos, recreational gambling is an increasingly popular way to spend a few hours. And more than a few dollars.

Venues vary from the plush to the plain:

▶Reno, Nev. Vegas' kid sister. 22 casino hotels, 23,865 rooms, 446 miles from the original.

In its back yard: Tahoe.

Lake Tahoe's sparkling cool water, its 75 miles of shoreline and 18 ski resorts nearby attract a different crowd. Gambling by night, pursuing great outdoor adventures by day.

▶Atlantic City. A workaday version of Vegas. Small bettors and day-trippers make up the bulk of the business. Forty million people within a day's drive or bus ride. Revenues rival the original, but are split among just 12 casino hotels.

▶North Dakota. No threat to Monaco, but willing to give gambling a chance. Allows casino-style blackjack rooms, but sets a $2 limit on bets.

Gov. George Sinner, 60, explained his state's low-budget blackjack: "I think the modest approach that's been taken here recognizes that it's perfectly all right for people to engage in recreational gambling. But that there are some real risks, and that, if you're going to move into the area, you might want to do it on a gradual basis, and feel your way along. That's essentially what's been done here and I think it's been very successful."

Sun and Sand

Florida was our finale.

The last state we visited. A place to work, yes, but also a place to set work aside. A place to stretch out. Sleep late. Swim a few slow laps. Get sunburned.

Every state works to attract tourists, but the Sunshine State has an advantage. To most of us, Florida is practically a synonym for rest and relaxation. An alternative spelling of vacation.

Central Florida alone hosts five of the USA's most popular theme parks:

►Sea World. 4 million annual guests.

►Spaceport, the visitors' complex at the Kennedy Space Center. 2.2 million annual guests.

►Cypress Gardens. 1.3 million.

►Wet'n'Wild. 1 million.

►And the king of them all: Walt Disney World. 20 million visitors annually. 19,500 employees.

Disney began the boom that turned Orlando into a magic kingdom for vacationers and the businesses that cater to them. Since Disney's 1971 opening:

►Orlando's population has doubled.

►Area hotel rooms have increased from 5,000 to nearly 60,000.

"Orlando is a busy, busy city," says resident Agnes Ferrell, a 51-year-old florist. "I've been to the 'Mouse's House' at least 75 times. The first 40 times, I really enjoyed it. Then it became a really good place to take all my guests."

But there's more to Florida than Mickey and Minnie. The staples of tourism remain the ocean, the beach, a better-than-even chance of getting a suntan.

Some find solitude and serenity along Florida's 1,997 miles of coast. We met Carol Lawing, a 37–year-old law student from Smyrna, Fla., combing the beach on Sanibel Island. "I'm a sea-shell fanatic," she told us. "Sanibel is one of the best places in the world to shell. . . . You find little beauties. It's like a treasure trove."

Others seek more raucous recreation. Especially the 525,000 college students who take part in a yearly ritual called Spring Break. Daytona businessman Bill Urff, 33, enjoys Spring Break as much as any college sophomore. He earns his living selling beer. "Everybody is happy during the Daytona 500 races and at Spring Break. During Spring Break, I sell as many kegs of beer in a day as I normally sell in one week. You'd be happy, too.''

Recreation Across the USA

Skiing. Fishing. Gambling. Tourism. And those only scratch the surface of how we use our free time. According to the Census Bureau:

▶44 percent garden.
▶41 percent swim.
▶33 percent bicycle.
▶23 percent jog.
▶22 percent play softball.

And whatever we do with our free time, we do more of it.

In short, the people of the USA are anything but leisurely about their leisure time. In their own words:

▶Beth Ciancaglini, 20, bank teller in Annapolis, Md., says she enjoys her hometown: ''Living here is like being on a permanent vacation. We have sailing, boating, water skiing, boat shows. I crab every morning before work.''

▶Juliana Moore, 17, a high school student in Wabaseka, Ark., has hunted since she was 6: ''My daddy dragged me along so he could kill my limit and his limit, too. I had to sit still and be quiet and not say anything. I like to hunt ducks, but it's usually cold and wet, and my waders always leak.''

▶Eric Bye, 39, an insurance salesman in Saxtons River, Vt., says he has found a special balance: ''I could have made a much better living somewhere else, but I've always been careful not to confuse my living with my life. In Vermont, we draw that distinction. I could strap on my skis in my back yard and ski to the Canadian border.''

Living here is like being on a permanent vacation. We have sailing, boating, water skiing, boat shows. I crab every morning before work.

BETH CIANCAGLINI

The Play Ethic

Not so long ago, a little leisure time was seen as a reward for a lot of hard work. Slack hours were few and far between.

Now recreation is seen as a necessity. A key to health and well-being.

While many of us still put in long hours at our jobs, we're working harder than ever at having fun. From Alaska's wide-open spaces to Disney World's Space Mountain, we met people who take the pursuit of happiness to heart.

10 THE STAR-SPANGLED BANNER STILL WAVES

Patriotism prevails. It's proof of pride in our nation. It shows in the way we preserve our past. In the way we protect our future.

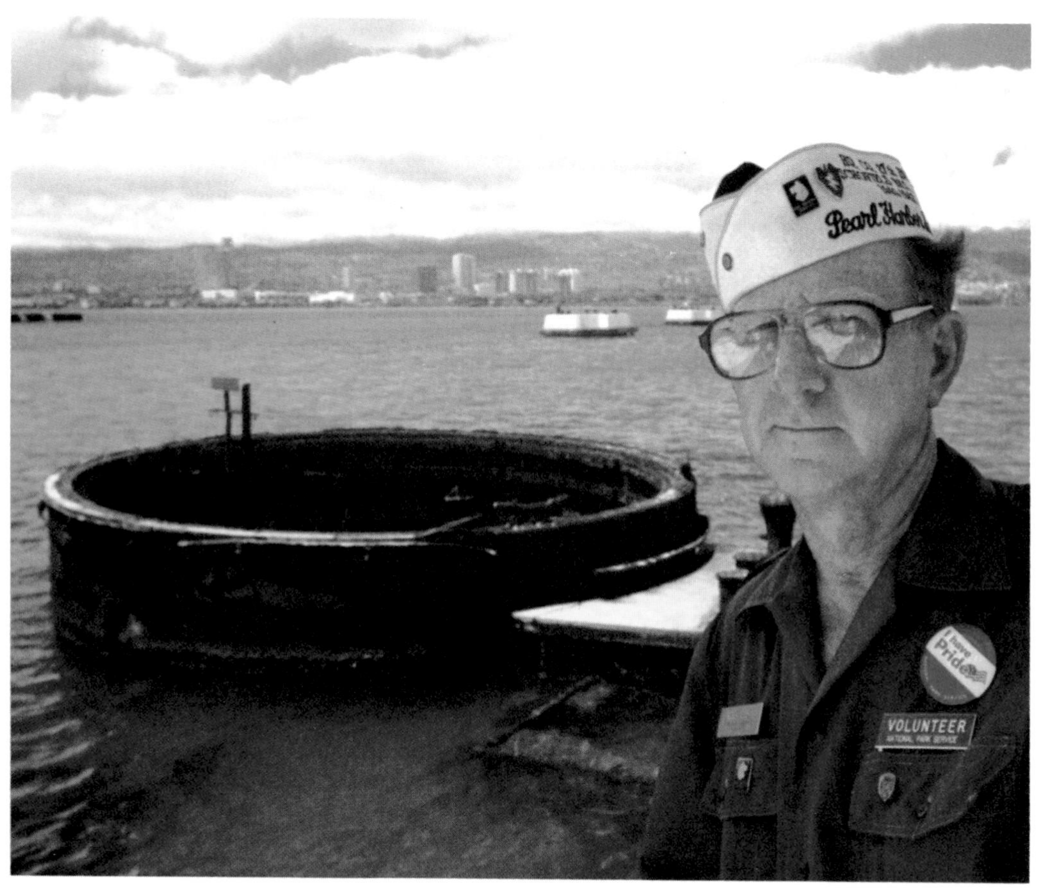

WAR MEMORIES: Veteran Bob Kinzler of Honolulu recalls how the bombing of Pearl Harbor challenged his courage and patriotism.

na and Julio Palma didn't mean to upstage the Magna Carta.

Nor did they intentionally overshadow the U.S. attorney general, the British princess or the other dignitaries assembled to kick off Philadelphia's celebration of the bicentennial of the Constitution.

But they couldn't help it.

Amid all the fanfare and famous faces, it was Ana and Julio, and others like them, who drew the most interest and excited the strongest emotions.

The crowds had gathered to salute the Magna Carta for its contribution to our Constitution and the protection of individual rights and liberties.

Ana and Julio had come to claim those rights. The young couple from El Salvador, holding their 20–month-old son, were among a group taking the oath of allegiance to the USA.

As the princess, the crowd and the BusCateers watched, Ana and Julio became citizens.

After the ceremony, Julio, 31, a die maker, told us his feelings: "This is the happiest day in our lives. It's our dream to become Americans."

We found that sentiment echoed time and again throughout our trip.

Displaying the flag is "in" again. Patriotism is alive and well across the USA.

But we also saw that it is changing.

In years gone by, patriotism usually meant marching in the parade on the Fourth of July. Saluting the flag. Fighting for your country.

Today, patriotism is often less obvious, less sentimental. Patriotism can show up in the ways we preserve our past. The values and ideals we embrace. The way we question our leaders and ourselves.

"But It's So Tiny"

"That's Plymouth Rock?"

"But it's so tiny. How could they land a ship on that?"

That was the reaction of two BusCateers looking for

the first time at one of the USA's most celebrated landmarks. Disappointment.

Plymouth Rock is a very modest monument.

A 4– or 5–foot-high boulder with "1620" carved on one side. Surrounded by an outsized structure reminiscent of a Greek temple.

But the little rock is eloquent in its own way.

It reminds us the USA wasn't a big, important country when the pilgrims landed here. It wasn't a country at all, but a wilderness.

And the arriving pilgrims weren't concerned with choosing monuments, but with getting ashore and getting to work. The time for monuments and sentiment would come later.

Traveling to numerous historic landmarks in the course of our trip, we realized that there are two types of tourists: the casual and the reverent.

For many, a trip to Plymouth Rock, Mass., is a fairly lighthearted excursion. For others, these landmarks are more compelling. Serious. Solemn.

For Ben Valdez, 65, of McAllen, Texas, the trip to Plymouth Rock was a pilgrimage.

A Cherokee Indian, he said his background made him more aware of how different this land was when the Puritans arrived. Plymouth Rock, to him, symbolized that bygone world.

"Plymouth Rock has special meaning to me," he told us. "That's why the country is the way it is. They improved it. And they had to suffer to come here."

"He's Always Referred to as Mr. Jefferson"

Virginia prizes its precedents and presidents.

The "mother of presidents" has sent eight favorite sons to the White House: Washington, Jefferson, Madison, Monroe, Harrison, Tyler, Taylor, Wilson.

But some sons are more favored than others.

And Thomas Jefferson may be the most favored of all.

Why Jefferson?

Why not Washington, father of our country? Or Madison, principal author of the Constitution? Or Wilson, organizer of the League of Nations?

Perhaps Jefferson's rivals are simply outnumbered. Jefferson's admirers dote on the depth and variety of his talents:

▶Literary genius, evidenced in the Declaration of Independence.

▶Exploring spirit, demonstrated by his sponsorship of explorers Lewis and Clark.

▶Architectural talent, embodied by his graceful and original design for his home, Monticello, near Charlottesville, Va.

▶Love of learning and belief in progress, exemplified in his founding of the University of Virginia.

Nowhere is Jefferson's presence more strongly felt than at the University of Virginia in Charlottesville, established by Jefferson in 1819.

Terry Wood, 41, a university administrator, told us, "The influence of Thomas Jefferson is amazing. You get the feeling he's behind a tree somewhere."

Edward Peterson, 29, doctoral student in art history at the university, said knowledge of Jefferson was practically a prerequisite for graduation here.

"You don't go to school in Virginia and not know who Jefferson is or what he represents."

We couldn't help noticing that Peterson used the present tense.

"The Most Heroic of Our Heroes"

George Washington was not boring.

That's what the curators and caretakers at Mount Vernon, Washington's family estate in Virginia, try to impress upon their visitors.

"George Washington is probably the most heroic of our heroes," said Jim Reeves, 35, acting director at Mount Vernon.

"He had a combination of talents that made him an effective leader. He was a hero in his own times," said Reeves.

He just has an image problem.

While nobody calls the father of our country dull, few seem as passionately intrigued by Washington as by other historical lights such as Thomas Jefferson or Abraham Lincoln.

Perhaps it's because he's been worn out.

Our first president has lent his name to:

- ▶More than 100 cities and towns, including the nation's capital.
- ▶10 lakes.
- ▶Eight streams.
- ▶Seven mountains.

His appearance on our currency adds to the familiarity. In 1987:

- ▶3,970,399,629 one-dollar bills were printed.
- ▶An estimated 15.2 billion quarters featuring his face were in circulation.

If shared traditions and ideas unify the USA, then Washington's fate is ironic but appropriate.

Nothing in our history is more widely known or widely shared than the name of George Washington.

Through the use of his name and image, Washington today continues the work he began more than 200 years ago. Drawing together people from across the nation. Helping us recognize our common concerns and realize our common goals. Uniting the country.

In return, perhaps the millions of us who carry his picture in our wallets should make an effort to think of him as a whole, real, complex human being.

After all, said Reeves: "He was much more interesting than people give him credit for. People think he was as flat as the dollar bill, but he had many different interests and ideas."

A Full-Time Ben Franklin

Statesman, scholar, scientist Ben Franklin looked fit and cheerful when he was interviewed by the Bus-Capade.

A little heavy around the middle, perhaps. A little thin on top. But, all in all, quite remarkable for a man of 281 years.

His secret?

An actor named Ralph Archbold.

Through his appearances in museums, at public events and just about anywhere, Archbold helps keep Franklin's spirit alive and lively in the city of Philadelphia.

"I'm not just an actor with a wig," said Ralph. "I'm a full-time Ben Franklin."

A natural physical resemblance and a careful re-creation of Franklin's personal style—from the long hair to the square, wire-rim spectacles—make Archbold a familiar face even to those who have never met him.

But this Ben Franklin is a little bit different. He's married to Betsy Ross.

As one group of BusCateers interviewed Ralph Archbold, 45, at City Hall, another team across town was visiting the former home of the USA's first flagmaker. Playing the part of Betsy Ross as she led a group of young tourists through the house was a talkative, friendly woman named Sue Archbold.

While Ralph performs daily as Ben Franklin, Sue, 32, works as a tour guide through the city's historic districts, performing as Betsy Ross on special occasions.

Theirs is a marriage made in history.

Sue told us her husband's occupation seems touched by fate: Both Franklin and Archbold were born on the same day, Jan. 17.

As for herself and Betsy Ross, she said there are one or two similarities: "She was a seamstress and a working mother. Similar to me."

Another parallel, said Sue, was a shared passion: "Of course I'm patriotic. My stars and garters, yes!"

Civil War

Fort Sumter, S.C.

Today, a grassy, restful national park.

On April 12, 1861, the scene of the first violence of the

Civil War when Confederate forces fired upon federal troops stationed here.

The war that began then lasted five years. Cost more than $15 billion. 529,332 lives. Northern and Southern.

BusCapade USA traveled to Fort Sumter the only way we could, the only way that any of the 1861 combatants could. By boat.

Floating across Charleston's calm harbor, past the peaceful parks and houses of this old brick city, it was hard to believe so much death and destruction began here.

Jack Dugan, 41, park ranger at Fort Sumter, told us the violent past is still recent enough to pose a danger to modern excavators.

Any time we dig a hole for a water main, we've got to be careful. We could dig up a live shell. That's a problem we have at Civil War sites—some of our artifacts are dangerous.

Live ammunition is just one part of the legacy of the Civil War that lives on here.

"It's still called The War," said Dugan. "There are still lots of old families in Charleston. Names you see in history books still live in the same houses that they did then. The memory is passed on from grandparents to grandchildren."

Gary McKinney, 34, is one of those grandchildren. Or great-grandchildren.

The husky native South Carolinian was taking his young family on an outing to Fort Sumter when we met him, teaching them about their ancestors who fought for the Confederacy. Passing on the memory.

He said repercussions of the war, and the beliefs behind it, are still visible in his home state.

"South Carolina still epitomizes the traditional South," he said. "The people are progressive in some ways, but they cling to the traditional Southern values. The bloodlines are deep. The same families have been here for hundreds of years."

He defends the secessionists for having the courage of their convictions.

"In the Civil War, people did what they felt they had

to do at the time. They believed in something and they fought for it and lost."

But McKinney has no desire for a rematch.

Both Dugan and McKinney, like others we interviewed throughout the South, said Southern separatism is a thing of the past.

While this region will always have a unique identity—and a sympathy for the Confederacy—both said the differences between North and South have been exaggerated in books, movies and the national imagination.

"I like to think we're all one country now, with unique parts in it," said McKinney. "You can't judge a person by his accent."

Later in the afternoon, as we were leaving the fort, Dugan summed up the Southern attitude toward the war.

"Despite the popularity of the Great Lost Cause," he said, smiling under the brim of his ranger's hat, "I think most of our visitors are pretty happy with the way things worked out."

Any time we dig a hole for a water main, we've got to be careful. We could dig up a live shell. That's a problem we have at Civil War sites—some of our artifacts are dangerous.

JACK DUGAN

"If I'm Called, I'm Ready to Go"

Pearl Harbor remembers.

Remembers the attack. Remembers the war.

Remembers the fear, passion and pride.

Ernie Haynes, 64, remembers. On Sunday, Dec. 7, 1941, Haynes was a corporal in the 251st Coast Artillery Regiment on Oahu in Hawaii.

"When I first heard those explosions," he told Bus-Capade, "it scared the bejesus out of me. I was going to sleep in, but that woke me up."

One image stands out in the confusion of that morning. An attacking plane swooping down on the barracks. Guns firing. A Japanese war emblem emblazoned on its side.

"When that Zero came in strafing us with machine guns, and we saw that big red meatball on the side, we realized what was going on."

Bob Kinzler, 65, also remembers. He was a private with the 27th Infantry Regiment based at Schofield Barracks.

He remembers the fear. "With the dropping of the first bombs, there was a tremendous explosion. I remember wondering who was doing it and why they were doing it. I wondered if it hurt to get shot and if I was going to die." It would be a hard day to forget:

▶2,334 U.S. military personnel died that day.
▶18 U.S. ships were sunk.
▶170 U.S. planes destroyed.
▶The USA declared war upon Japan the next day.

Forty years later, the Japanese are back at Pearl Harbor; 22,265 Hawaii residents were born in Japan. Other Japanese are here vacationing, investing, remembering.

Nearly a million Japanese visit here annually.

Kinzler was talking to a group of tourists at the USS Arizona Memorial when we met him. Since his retirement, he has worked there part time as a volunteer tour guide.

Several Japanese tourists were among those asking about his memories and experiences. Many took photographs of him. Some had their picture taken with him.

Kinzler told us that remembering is different from holding a grudge.

"I have no animosity toward them now," he said. "I've lived with them in Hawaii for years. You can't hold a grudge and live next to someone for 30 years."

More durable than hatred are the courage and commitment that were tested by the war. Kinzler not only remembers his patriotic feelings, he feels just as passionately about them today.

"I'm old enough so that I can sit back and relax and enjoy life. I can ride on the bus for free," he told us, squinting into the sun. "But if I'm called, I'm ready to go."

Easy Rider

Christine Jones, 27, was following a time-honored tradition when we met her near Ames, Iowa.

Hitting the road.

Looking for the heart and soul of the country.

She was heading north, riding in the breakdown lane.

She wasn't broken down, but we would have understood if she was.

Instead, she was riding on the shoulder to avoid the gusts from passing cars and trucks as she pedaled her heavy-laden 10–speed bicycle up the gradient and through the 100–degree Iowa summer.

Her plastic helmet, rear-view mirror and neoprene biking pants told us that she was a serious cyclist on an extended trip. But we didn't see any traveling companions.

Curious about this lone rider, we pulled over and flagged her down.

"It's a personal adventure," she told us between drinks from her water bottle. "I wanted some solitude."

And she wanted some reassurance.

She wanted her faith in people, and in the USA, to be restored. A native of Philadelphia, she had left a job in a New York bank, disappointed by the goals and values she had seen there. She hoped to find something more worthy, more humane and enduring, on the road.

And her hope was fulfilled.

"After living in the East and working on Wall Street," she said, "it's nice to see there are still good, friendly, trustworthy people.

"Every little town you go into, people take you into their houses and give you dinner," she told us. "The moral fabric is still out there."

Patriotism Across the USA

Others we met on the road agreed with Christine Jones.

The USA is still a special country.

There are still good people and worthy ideas in this country.

There are still reasons to be proud of our country.

That pride is one of the ties that bind us to each other.

Across the USA, people white and black, rich and

poor, English-speaking and Spanish-speaking, share the common ground of pride and patriotism.

▶Juanita Bacon, 57, Hutchinson, Kan., told us planting and harvesting the amber waves of grain on her family's farm made her conscious of the USA's natural blessings.

"There's so much pride when you see rich dark rows of wheat," she said. "First you see little green shoots. It's like a beautiful green carpet. Then comes this beautiful, waving golden wheat. It makes you want to sing *The Star-Spangled Banner*."

▶Ken Carr, 36, computer engineer, Mason City, Iowa, said his town had been the model for River City in Meredith Willson's beloved musical *The Music Man*. He told us the sweetness and good nature of the city in the play are based on reality.

"This is the heartland," he said. "This is what we go to war to protect. There's an innocence to this part of the country. It shows up in the schoolkids' faces. To us, it's easier to be optimistic than cynical.

"We were brought up to be patriotic. There are usually parades on the Fourth of July. When you see a dad at a parade with his boy on his shoulders—what else is there?"

We were brought up to be patriotic. There are usually parades on the Fourth of July. When you see a dad at a parade with his boy on his shoulders—what else is there?
KEN CARR

▶Heather McKie, 10, Jackson, Miss., was touring Philadelphia with a school group when we met her.

"I like Philadelphia because it's important to know what happened a long time ago," said the shy, blond fifth-grader.

"When they wrote the Constitution they were thinking about how it would affect the people in the future. They wanted our freedom to last forever, and we still have all of it."

A visit to the former house of Betsy Ross had inspired her to want to make a contribution: "If we ever have to build a new flag, I'd like to make it."

The USA today is in a patriotic mood.

That may not be news—advertising agencies have been using this knowledge to sell beer, trucks and hamburgers for several years—but few seem to understand the nature of today's patriotism.

Today's patriotism grows from a renewed sense of pride in the USA's history and ideas.

Not from a rekindled wish to win the Vietnam War. Nor any strong desire to flex our muscle elsewhere in the world.

The patriots we met were homey, friendly people. Farmers, actors, college administrators. The fighters were few and far between.

Even the warriors we met—the guards at the Tomb of the Unknown Soldier, the World War II veterans in Hawaii—thought restraint and maturity the better part of valor.

The patriots we met celebrated practical virtues and humane ideals:

▶The determination of the Puritans.
▶The public spirit of George Washington.
▶The learning and wisdom of Thomas Jefferson.
▶The hope of Ana and Julio Palma.

Patriotism today is not just a thirst for glory, but a sense of responsibility.

The *Star-Spangled Banner* still waves. But not just in the rockets' red glare. It waves every day, everywhere as a symbol of pride and hope—to our fellow citizens, our country, our world, our future.

11 THE USA TOMORROW

The promise of tomorrow brings bright prospects. We combine courage and character, pride and passion as we focus on the future.

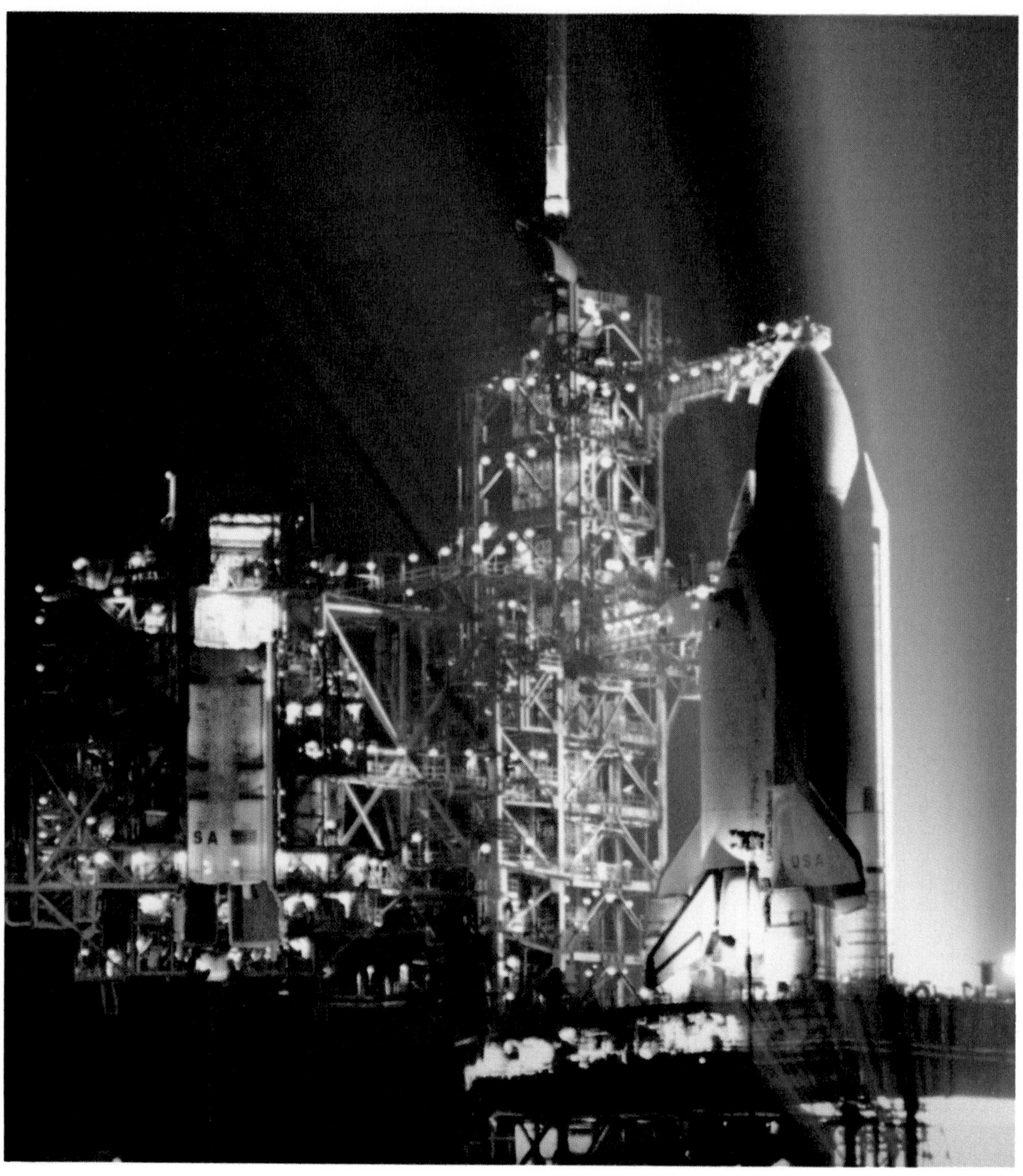

FUTURE FOCUS: Today's technology focuses on tomorrow at the Kennedy Space Center in Cape Canaveral, Fla., our gateway to the universe.

ur last stop was the White House.

Six months and 34,905 miles after setting out, we parked the bus at 1600 Pennsylvania Ave., turned off the ignition. Jotted down the number on the odometer.

Our Oval Office interview with President Reagan completed our coverage. After the president, we had only ourselves to question.

What had we learned?

Has the dream of the USA been fulfilled?

Is it over?

Is the future a thing of the past?

From Anchorage to Atlanta . . .

From bartenders and bishops . . .

From school children and senior citizens . . .

. . . we found passionate opinions about the USA's prospects. Some were somber. Most were full of hope and anticipation.

Concerns and challenges? Of course. But with the pioneers and promise to solve them.

Across the USA, most people dwell not on yesterday. There is some concentration on today. But the real focus is on tomorrow.

One hundred and fifty years ago, Ralph Waldo Emerson compared history-loving Europe with a forward-looking USA. Here, he wrote:

"The past is prologue."

And so it is in the USA today.

The past is our prologue to the future.

The USA tomorrow surely offers even more hope and opportunity than the USA of yesterday or today.

AUTHORS

Allen H. Neuharth, 64, is chairman of Gannett Co. Inc. and founder of USA TODAY, The Nation's Newspaper. A native of South Dakota, Neuharth joined the Associated Press in 1950. Later he launched his first newspaper, a statewide South Dakota weekly called *SoDak Sports*, which failed financially.

He then worked as a reporter, editor and news executive for Knight newspapers in Miami and Detroit for 10 years. He joined Gannett in 1963, became president in 1970, chief executive officer in 1973 and chairman in 1979.

He is also the author of *Plain Talk Across the USA* and *Profiles of Power: How the Governors Run Our 50 States*, both published by USA TODAY Books.

Kenneth A. Paulson, 34, has been a reporter and editor with Gannett for 10 years. Paulson was the editor of the *Green Bay* (Wis.) *Press-Gazette*, managing editor of the *Bridgewater* (N.J.) *Courier News*, and began his career as a reporter for the *Fort Myers* (Fla.) *News-Press*. He was a member of USA TODAY's start-up staff.

An attorney and member of the Illinois and Florida bars, Paulson is chief of staff and special assistant to Neuharth. He is the co-author of *Profiles of Power: How the Governors Run Our 50 States*.

Daniel J. Greaney, 24, has been a reporter with Gannett for two years. A former president of the *Harvard Lampoon*, Greaney was editor of the *Lampoon's* 1986 parody of USA TODAY.

ABOUT THIS BOOK

This book is based on interviews conducted during USA TODAY's 50-state, 34,905-mile BusCapade from March 16 to Sept. 10, 1987.

More than 3,000 people were interviewed by the BusCapade news team and correspondents throughout the USA.

Joining the authors on the nation's highways and byways:

▶Lou Brancaccio, 38, managing editor of the Fort Myers, Fla. *News-Press* and a BusCapade editor.

▶Paula Burton, 27, a producer with WXIA-TV in Atlanta and a BusCapade reporter.

▶Lisa Dixon, 33, a promotion/market research director with *The* (Wilmington, Del.) *News-Journal*, who coordinated press relations on BusCapade.

▶Joel Driver, 29, BusCapade bus driver.

▶Gaynelle Evans, 36, a Gannett News Service and BusCapade reporter.

▶Scott Maclay, 38, a corporate staff member and BusCapade photographer.

▶Juanie Phinney, 24, executive secretary and BusCapade logistics assistant.

▶Phil Pruitt, 37, a corporate staff member who coordinated interviews with the USA's governors.

▶Barbara Reynolds, 46, USA TODAY Inquiry page editor, who participated in many BusCapade interviews with governors and celebrities.

▶Bob Roller, 27, a corporate staff member and BusCapade photographer.

▶David Silk, 23, a USA TODAY circulation manager and BusCapade logistics assistant.

▶Kathleen Smith Barry, 29, *The* (Nashville) *Tennessean* and BusCapade photographer.

Gannett President and Chief Executive John Curley, USA TODAY Editor John Quinn, USA TODAY Executive Editor Ron Martin, USA TODAY Editorial Director

John Seigenthaler, USA TODAY Publisher Cathleen Black, USA TODAY President Thomas Curley, Gannett Vice President/News Charles Overby, and Gannett Vice President/Public Affairs and Government Relations Mimi Feller provided special support throughout BusCapade.

The Gannett New Media staff helped design, edit and publish this book: Nancy Woodhull, Gannett vice president/news services and president of Gannett New Media, and Phil Fuhrer, Emilie Davis, Robert C. Gabordi, J. Ford Huffman, Randy Kirk, Rebecca Conroy, Lark Borden, Theresa Klisz Harrah, Bill Beene, Mary Demby, Carolynne Miller, Shelley Beaudry, Anita Sama, Leslie Lapides, Bert Gustavson, Susan Lynch, Kent Travis, Tom Snoreck, Bill Perry, Ann LaRose, Maggie Somerville, Bill Librizzi and Beth Goodrich.

JoAn Moore provided valuable technical assistance.

We thank them all.

AL NEUHARTH, KEN PAULSON, DAN GREANEY